HODDER 20TH CENTURY HISTORY

THE COLD WAR AND AFTER
SECOND EDITION

CONTENTS

Key Issue

Who was to blame for the start of the Cold War, 1945–9?

ORIGINS OF THE COLD WAR

When the Second World War ended in 1945, most European countries were in ruins or exhausted by six years of fighting. Countries that had once been powerful now needed peace to rebuild themselves. Only two **superpowers** remained after 1945 – the USA and the USSR.

They had fought the war together as allies. They had shared victory together. Yet, afterwards, they did not completely trust each other. This distrust never led to fighting between the two countries but there were regular quarrels. Historians call this period the 'Cold War'.

The reasons for this distrust went back to long before the Second World War. In 1917, the Russian Revolution had put communists in power in Russia. (They had changed its name to USSR in 1924.) Soon afterwards, countries such as Britain and the USA helped the communists' opponents during a civil war. From then on, the Russians did not trust the Americans and the Americans did not trust the Russians.

STALIN'S FEARS

The Soviet Union wanted to spread communism. American leaders were afraid that the USSR would try to start communist revolutions elsewhere in the world, including in the United States itself.

The USSR's leader was Joseph Stalin. He did not trust the USA or Britain to protect the USSR. It was 1933 before the USA recognised the Soviet Union. For most of the 1930s, neither Britain nor the USA supported him against Hitler. Stalin had become convinced that the West intended to let Hitler destroy the USSR.

Because the USSR was the only communist country, Stalin felt isolated. He was worried that **capitalist** countries might use their money to attack the Soviet Union.

In 1941, the USSR was attacked by a capitalist country – Nazi Germany led by Adolf Hitler. The USSR fought alongside the USA and Britain to defeat Hitler but it cost at least 20 million Soviet lives. Stalin urged the British and the Americans to open the 'second front' by invading German-occupied France in 1943. This would help the Soviet Union because the Germans would have to move troops from the Eastern Front in the USSR to deal with the **Allies** in France. Stalin was bitter that the western Allies did not invade Europe until June, 1944. He was still convinced that they wanted to destroy **communism**.

As his **Red Army** pushed back the German armies in 1942–5, Stalin was determined that his country would be secure in future. He believed the

The differences between the Soviet communist system and the American capitalist system also made the two countries frightened of each other.

USSR had to organise its own defence. One way of doing this was to ensure that neighbouring countries were friendly towards the USSR, and therefore unlikely to attack. Stalin decided that this meant they had to become communist as well.

In 1945, Britain and the USA could not stop him doing this. By then, nearly all of eastern Europe was under the Red Army's control.

YALTA

From 4–11 February 1945, 'the Big Three' – Churchill (representing Britain), President Roosevelt (USA) and Stalin (USSR) – held a **summit meeting** at Yalta in the Soviet Union. Stalin wanted Germany to pay huge **reparations** to cover the damage that the Germans had done in the Soviet Union.

Churchill and Roosevelt did not think it sensible to punish Germany so severely but Stalin was determined. So they agreed that the USSR would get reparations in goods. The Russians took factory equipment and other materials out of Germany and Austria and took them back to the USSR. At the same time, many East Germans were put in **labour camps** and forced to work for the Russians.

The other main decisions taken at Yalta were:

- Germany would be **demilitarised** and divided into four zones, each controlled by one Allied power – the USSR, USA, Britain and France.
- The city of Berlin would also be divided between the four powers.
- Eastern Europe should be under Soviet influence.
- In return, Stalin accepted that Britain would have influence over Greece.
- The USSR gained land from eastern Poland. Poland would gain land from Germany in return.
- Germans who were guilty of war crimes would be put on trial.
- All countries freed from the Germans could choose their own democratic government in free elections.
- Stalin agreed to join the new **United Nations** organisation.
- The USSR would join in the war against Japan soon after Germany surrendered.

POTSDAM

Despite the distrust, Stalin and Roosevelt got on well at Yalta – but it was the last time they met. In April 1945, Roosevelt died and Harry Truman became American President. On 7 May 1945, Germany surrendered and the war in Europe ended. Truman trusted Stalin much less than Roosevelt had.

The Allies next met at Potsdam on 17 July – 1 August 1945. During this conference, Churchill learned that he had lost the general election. The new Prime Minister, Attlee, took over as the British representative on July 27. He shared Truman's attitude to Stalin.

Something else happened during the Potsdam Conference. Truman learned that the atomic bomb had been successfully tested. He told Stalin that the USA had developed a new weapon, but Stalin may not have realised how important this was. In any case, Truman did not tell Stalin that he was about to drop an atomic bomb on Japan.

A SOURCE

A French cartoon showing Stalin gradually taking over China and the countries of eastern Europe.

Questions

a Describe the key decisions made at Yalta in 1945. [6 marks]

b What does Source A tell us about France's fears in the years immediately after 1945? [3 marks]

c How reliable is Source A to an historian studying developments in Europe after 1945? [6 marks]

2 THE USSR AND POLAND

Key Issue

- What was the Iron Curtain?

THE ODER–NEISSE LINE

Some new decisions were made at Potsdam. The British and Americans agreed that the USSR could take 30% of the industrial equipment from the western zones of Germany as **reparations**. They also allowed the USSR to send all Germans living in Poland, Hungary and Czechoslovakia back to Germany.

But the key agreement concerned Poland. At Yalta, Poland's western boundary had not been finally fixed. Before the Potsdam Conference, Stalin privately agreed with the Poles to position it along the Rivers Oder and Neisse. (It became known as the Oder–Neisse Line.) This was further west than either the Allies or the Germans wanted.

Key
- - - - - 1939 pre-war boundary / German land gained by Poland
———— Post-Potsdam boundary / Polish land gained by the USSR

Germany and Poland, showing the new border, after the Potsdam Conference.

POLAND'S 'FREE' ELECTIONS

However, Stalin repeated his promise that there would be free elections in Poland. Poland was important because British support for Poland had led to war. Polish elections were held – but in reality they were far from free.

As early as 1941, the USSR had parachuted communists into Poland to fight the **fascists** and promote **communism**. Meanwhile, the Polish government had gone into exile in London.

In 1943, there was conflict between the USSR and the Polish government. The USSR broke off all relations with it and set up a rival 'National Committee' in Moscow.

In the summer of 1944, the **Red Army** began liberating Poland. By July, the communist National Committee had set itself up at Lublin, the first major city to be freed.

In February 1945, at Yalta, the 'Big Three' agreed that the USA and Britain would accept the National Committee as the Polish government, provided that representatives of the London government were also included. In particular, they wanted the non-communist People's Party leader to be included. They also agreed that democratic Polish elections would be held that same year.

Just three months later, the communists took action. Sixteen nationalist (non-communist) **resistance** leaders were arrested and a new government was formed. It included the People's Party leader as Deputy Prime Minister.

No elections were held in 1945. Instead, the country found itself practically fighting a civil war. Non-communist **partisans** fought a **guerrilla war** against communist security forces. A propaganda war was launched against the People's Party. By the summer of 1946, 1200 of their members had been arrested. And there were still no elections.

The elections finally took place in January 1947. By then, the communists had locked up about 100,000 members of the People's Party – as well as 142 election candidates.

At the election, communists frightened voters into voting for communist candidates. To no one's

Communist propaganda on Polish stamps.

surprise, they won the election, winning 394 seats out of the 444. The 'free, democratic election' was over: the government that Stalin wanted had been elected.

THE IRON CURTAIN

In March 1946, Winston Churchill gave a speech in President Truman's home state, Missouri. He summed up his attitude towards the USSR and introduced a phrase that became famous – the 'Iron Curtain' (see Source A).

Churchill wanted a new Anglo-American alliance against the USSR. In fact, Truman did not support this. Nor did most Americans want it. They still hoped that the USA and USSR would co-operate as they had during the war. But Churchill's speech made Stalin angry and, a week later, he replied (see Source B).

Winston Churchill giving his famous 'Iron Curtain' speech.

A SOURCE

Winston Churchill, speaking at Fulton in Missouri (March, 1946).

From Stettin in the Baltic to Trieste in the Adriatic, an Iron Curtain has descended across the continent. Behind that line lie all the capitals of the ancient states of central and eastern Europe. All these famous cities and the populations around them lie in the Soviet sphere and all are subject not only to Soviet influence but to a very high measure of control from Moscow.

B SOURCE

Joseph Stalin, quoted in *Pravda* (13 March 1946).

There can be no doubt that Mr Churchill's position is a call for a war on the USSR.

The Soviet Union's loss of life has been several times greater than that of Britain and the United States put together. The Soviet Union cannot forget them. And so what is surprising that the Soviet Union, anxious for its future safety, is trying to ensure that governments loyal to the Soviet Union should exist in these countries?

C SOURCE

This British cartoon had the title: 'A Peep under the Iron Curtain' (1946).

Questions

a Study Source C. Explain the message of this cartoon. Support your answer by referring to details of the cartoon and your own knowledge. [6 marks]

b Explain why there was tension between Britain and the USSR at this time. [9 marks]

c Explain how the following contributed to tension between the Allies in 1945:
  • The delay in opening the Second Front
  • Poland
  • The atomic bomb.
  [10 marks]

3 THE COMMUNISTS TAKE CONTROL

Key Issue

How did the Soviet Union extend its control?

'A TORRENT OF LAVA'

Stalin was determined that the USSR should not be invaded again. What he wanted was a '**buffer zone**' of friendly countries between the USSR and Germany. The Second World War made this zone possible.

The USSR had suffered much during the war. From 1941–4, only the Soviet **Red Army** faced Germany on the mainland. By 1945, the Soviet Union had lost 20 million people.

From 1944 to April 1945, Soviet troops pushed German troops westwards across Europe. 'The Red Army was like a torrent of lava,' said a Soviet newspaper. By April 1945, it controlled almost all of eastern Europe. Soviet troops had reached Berlin itself. Stalin did not intend to give up the land that he had gained: this would be his buffer zone to protect the USSR.

Estonia, Latvia and Lithuania had become part of the USSR in 1940. At Yalta in 1945, the 'Big Three' had agreed that the USSR should keep part of Poland. Stalin also took land from Finland, Romania and Czechoslovakia. As a result, the USSR gained about 25 million people. More importantly, its border moved 300 miles west of where it had been in 1939.

ELECTIONS – SOVIET-STYLE

Stalin had his buffer zone – but he wanted more than just friendly neighbours; he wanted communist ones. Naturally, local communists had welcomed Soviet troops. In return, Stalin gave local communist parties his support.

During 1944–5, a few important communists went home to their liberated countries. They had spent the war in Moscow, where they had been trained by the Soviet Communist Party. What happened next in countries freed by the Red Army followed a pattern.

First, the communists joined in a **coalition government** – but they took the key jobs, such as running the police and the army.

Next, the communists got rid of the opposition. Fascists and capitalists were tried or expelled. Doubts were cast on non-communist politicians. Bit by bit, the opposition was whittled away.

Finally, an election was held when hardly any opponents were left. The candidates were all or mostly communists. When a communist government was elected, a '**people's democracy**' was set up. Its key people were those same communists who had been trained in the Soviet Union.

SOVIET TAKE-OVER OF HUNGARY

For example, the Red Army entered Hungary in September 1944. Free elections were held in November 1945 and they were won by the non-communist Smallholders' Party. In 1945–6, under Soviet pressure, secret police 'found evidence' against the Smallholders' Party and it lost power.

The United Workers' Party took over. Its leader was Mátyás Rákosi. He had been trained in Moscow during the war. Under his leadership, Hungary became a 'People's Republic' in 1949. It was given a new **constitution**, based on the Soviet Union's. Rákosi described the whole process as 'like slicing off salami'. He meant to remove his opponents, one by one, until there was no opposition left.

Hungary was not alone. One by one, the countries bordering the USSR became friendly communist neighbours. By March 1948, Stalin had also set up communist governments in Poland, East Germany, Romania, Bulgaria and Czechoslovakia. In each country, non-communist leaders had fled, been put in prison or were dead. In all of them, people were afraid to talk openly (see Source A).

YUGOSLAVIA DEFIES STALIN

But one resistance leader stood up to Stalin. He was Josip Broz, a communist resistance leader in Yugoslavia. He was better known as 'Tito'. His **partisan** army played the main role in forcing

'**Democracy**' in action: a Democratic Party gunman threatens the Romanian opposition in Bucharest.

The new map of Europe, 1948.

the Germans out of the country. When war ended, he was already head of a new government. He was successful and popular: it meant he could stand up to Stalin.

A split was inevitable and it happened in 1948. Tito refused to accept Stalin's orders and Stalin accused him of being a traitor. Yugoslavia was expelled from the Cominform. (In 1947, the USSR had set up the Communist Information Bureau, better known as Cominform. In theory, this provided information to all communist parties. In fact, Stalin used it to keep communist **satellites** under his control.) Stalin also cut off Soviet aid, hoping to force Tito to obey him. He failed: Yugoslavia became the only European communist country that was independent of the USSR.

'PEOPLE'S DEMOCRACIES'

In 1943, the 'Big Three' agreed that some of the eastern European countries could have governments friendly to the USSR after the war. And Stalin had warned Roosevelt that democracy in eastern Europe would not be the same as American democracy. This message did not at first sink in. 'People's democracies' were not what Roosevelt or Churchill had planned at Yalta.

Then, Churchill had been content to let Stalin have influence in Bulgaria, Romania and Hungary. However, the Red Army had advanced far faster than he had predicted or wanted. The Soviet 'empire' was greater than he had expected.

A SOURCE

Miroslav Mansfeld was a Czech who fought in the RAF during the war. Afterwards, he returned to Czechoslovakia. He described how it had changed (1991).

Before the war, you could speak openly in Czech against anything the Germans had done. [When] the Germans came, you couldn't speak. In 1946, after the election, you couldn't even speak to your friend about it. You just kept mum.

In 1945, people across the street would wave and greet you. After 1946, everybody just walked, didn't see anybody else. People were very frightened – they didn't know who was on the other side. There was just one year after the war when people could say what they liked to their oppressors. Then, a year later, it was 'Yes, master'.

1949: Newly communist countries (Czechoslovakia and Romania) celebrated Stalin's 70th birthday by issuing stamps with his face on.

Questions

a Explain what is meant by 'the Big Three'. [3 marks]

b Why was the Soviet Union able to secure control of much of eastern Europe after the end of the Second World War? [6 marks]

Key Issue

- How did the Truman Doctrine affect the Cold War?

CIVIL WAR IN GREECE

At Yalta, the 'Big Three' had agreed that Britain would have influence in Greece, and Stalin kept his word. In the Greek election of 1946, the communists were heavily defeated by **royalists** but the communists refused to give up.

They fought a **guerrilla war** against the Greek government and neighbouring communist countries sent help. Britain had 40,000 troops stationed in the country and gave money to the Greek government. It also gave money to the Turkish government, which was under Soviet pressure.

By 1947, Britain could no longer afford this. In February, the British government told the USA that they would have to pull out of Greece and stop helping Turkey.

After the war, the USA had played little part in European affairs. American troops had stayed in Germany but the rest had been sent back to the States. In March 1947, President Truman completely changed this policy. On 12 March 1947 he told Congress that:

'The United States has received from the Greek government an urgent appeal for financial and economic assistance. The very existence of the Greek State is today under threat from the terrorist activities of several thousand armed men, led by communists. The United States must supply this assistance.'

So far, his speech was asking Congress for support just in Greece. But Truman went on to explain why the issue was so important:

'One way of life is based upon the will of the majority, and is distinguished by free institutions, representative government, free elections, guarantees of individual liberty, freedom of speech and religion, and freedom from political oppression.

'The second way of life is based upon the will of a minority forcibly imposed upon the majority. It relies upon terror and oppression, a controlled press and radio, fixed elections, and the suppression of personal freedoms.

'I believe that it must be the policy of the United States to support free peoples who are resisting attempted subjugation by armed minorities or by outside pressures.'

Truman ended by asking for $400 million to help Greece and Turkey. Congress agreed. Less than three years later, the Greek communists gave up their struggle.

This Greek woman is telling an occupying army officer that she was forced to join the guerrillas.

CHANGE IN POLICY

Truman had announced a major change in American policy. The idea that the USA should help countries defeat **communism** became known as the 'Truman Doctrine'. In effect, the USA was taking on the role of the world's policeman in an attempt to stop communism spreading. The new American policy was to contain communism. One of the ways of doing this would be to give help to poor countries, because Truman believed that poor people were more likely to support the communists.

'THE COLD WAR'

Just days after Truman's speech, the USSR and the western powers failed to reach an agreement over Germany. In April, a US special adviser, called Bernard Baruch, gave a speech in South Carolina. At the time, Congress was discussing the Truman Doctrine. Baruch described the new relationship between the USA and the USSR. For the first time in public, he spoke of a 'cold war'.

That same year, President Truman set up the Central Intelligence Agency (**CIA**). Its job was to collect secret information and to undermine the USA's opponents. That meant the USSR, in particular.

THE MARSHALL PLAN

A German poster advertising the Marshall Plan.

Events now moved fast. In June, General George Marshall, the new US Secretary of State, announced an ambitious plan. It would provide American money to help the countries of Europe to recover from the war. He believed Europe needed this money if it was to stand up to the USSR. He also knew that the USA needed to trade with European countries. If Europe could not afford to buy American goods, American industry might go into a recession.

Britain's Foreign Secretary, Ernest Bevin, was very enthusiastic. Within days, he was organising a European response to the plan. Countries interested in the offer included Poland and Czechoslovakia. But, in July, the USSR condemned the plan. Soviet politicians claimed that the USA was using its money to put pressure on other countries.

Czechoslovakia agreed to attend talks with Marshall until Stalin called the Czech Prime Minister to Moscow. Poland turned down Marshall's offer. So did Finland, which was afraid of upsetting the USSR.

Marshall toured Europe to find out how much money was needed and came up with the figure of $13,000 million. Truman asked Americans to go without meat on Tuesdays and eggs on Thursdays to help Europe.

Then, in February 1948, communists overthrew the government of Czechoslovakia. Truman persuaded Congress that the aid was essential to stop communist revolutions elsewhere in Europe.

The Marshall Plan was a big success. The aid came in the form of goods, loans or even gifts until 1952. Food poured in; US machinery helped European factories to get back to normal; advisers helped to rebuild transport systems.

In western Europe, a European Recovery Programme (ERP) was set up. In 1948, this led to the Organisation for European Economic Co-operation (OEEC).

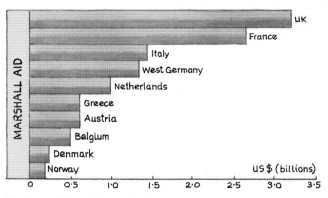

How Marshall Plan aid was shared out.

A SOURCE

A British cartoon of 1947 from *Punch* magazine. It shows Truman, with the cap in his hand, on the left, and Stalin pushing 'Hungary' onto the Russian bus.

THE RIVAL BUSES

Questions

a **Study Source A. Explain the message of this cartoon. Support your answer by referring to details of the cartoon and your own knowledge. [6 marks]**

b **Explain why the USA introduced the Marshall Plan. [9 marks]**

Key Issue

Why was the Berlin Airlift necessary?

BERLIN CUT OFF

In 1945, Germany was divided into four zones and so was Berlin, its capital. The city was 100 miles inside the Russian zone of Germany; it was linked to the west by road, rail and air routes.

Stalin wanted Germany to stay weak and divided because a weak Germany was no threat to the USSR. Britain, France and the USA wanted Germany to be prosperous once more. While Germany remained poor, the Allies had to give food and money to the people. On the other hand, a wealthier Germany would be a stronger Germany: it could become western Europe's first line of defence against the USSR.

In the winter of 1947–8, the USA, USSR, France and Britain discussed the idea of introducing a new currency in Germany. However, the talks got nowhere because the USSR was totally against the idea. In June 1948, the western powers decided to go ahead anyway. A new currency called the Deutschmark was introduced into their three zones.

The four zones of Berlin and the air corridors which connected Berlin with western Germany.

It was not used in western Berlin in case this caused problems with the Russians – but problems came anyway. The USSR decided to introduce its own currency into East Germany, including East Berlin. The West retaliated by introducing the Deutschmark into western Berlin.

While these disagreements went on, the USSR decided to force the western Allies out of Berlin. In the middle of June, the main **autobahn** into West Berlin was closed for repairs. At 6.00 am on 24 June, the USSR stopped all rail traffic between Berlin and western Germany.

West Berlin was surrounded by Soviet troops: the city was cut off. It was also short of power: gas, coal and electric supplies from East Berlin were stopped.

Two million people lived in West Berlin; unless the western powers helped them, they would starve within weeks. But what could the west do? General Clay, the governor of the American sector, wanted to send an armed convoy along the autobahn to force its way into Berlin. The Allies rejected the idea.

THE AIRLIFT BEGINS

Lieutenant Gail Halvorsen dropped thousands of sweets a day for Berlin children. The photograph shows him fitting them to parachutes made of handkerchiefs.

However, there was one other possibility: the air routes were still open. Of course, the Russians might try to shoot down aeroplanes but the USA thought it was unlikely. After all, the USA had atom bombs – the USSR did not. So, on 26 June, the first planes landed at Templehof Airport in western Berlin. They carried a few tons of tinned food and mail.

It was more a gesture than anything else. The West Berliners needed a minimum of 5000 tons of food and other essential supplies every day. Existing food stocks were expected to last for just 36 days. The USSR did not think that an airlift could supply everything that was needed. Even western reporters did not think an airlift would help the Berliners for long.

On 2 July, the rescue operation got properly under way. The British codenamed it 'Operation Plainfare'. It was the start of the biggest air operation in history. Soon, planes were flying day and night along the air corridors. Eventually, they were landing at 90-second intervals. Each was given an exact time; late planes had to return without landing.

The pilots had a dangerous job: Soviet planes flew across the air corridors and weather balloons were placed in awkward positions. But Stalin always stopped short of closing the air corridors. He did not want to risk a war.

By September, the planes were flying in 4600 tons of supplies a day – but it was still not enough. Meanwhile, the USSR tried to persuade the people of West Berlin to go and live in East Berlin. They were offered fresh vegetables, coal and bigger rations. All they had to do was register in the East. Less than 3 per cent of them took up the offer.

In West Berlin itself, civilians coped with the crisis. Food was rationed and each motorist was given just five gallons of petrol for a month. The subway trains and trams had stopped running.

The USSR hoped for a bad winter. Severe ice and snow would have limited flights; extreme cold would have killed the old and sick in the city. But the really bad weather never came. By January, Stalin knew his plan had failed.

The airlift brought more than food. These were some of the extras which were flown in.

2000 hot water bottles

Ping-pong balls

Steamroller

Manhole covers

A goat from the Royal Welsh Fusiliers

Dog for a blind man

THE AIRLIFT ENDS

The airlift continued into the spring. It reached a peak on 16–17 April 1949 when 1398 flights landed nearly 13,000 tons of supplies in 24 hours. By then, Stalin was seeking a way out.

The USSR ended its **blockade** of West Berlin at midnight on 12 May 1949. That evening, West Berliners put on evening dress and danced in the streets at the end of the autobahn. They were waiting for the red and white pole to be lifted, allowing the first car through.

This airlift memorial now stands at Templehof Airport, Berlin.

A SOURCE

This Soviet view of the airlift was given in *Soviet Foreign Policy* by Ilya Kremer (1968).

*The Soviet military government was forced to take emergency measures to protect the life and currency of East Germany. Checks were made on travellers coming from West Germany in order to keep out **speculators** and **profiteers**.*

The Soviet authorities were ready to provide food and fuel for the population of the whole of Berlin. However, the western occupying powers deprived the inhabitants of West Berlin of the possibility of obtaining any help from East Germany.

Questions

a Describe how the Western powers responded to Stalin's decision to blockade Berlin in 1948. [6 marks]

b What does Source A tell us about relations between the Western powers and the Soviet Union during the Blockade? [3 marks]

RESULTS OF THE AIRLIFT

The Berlin Airlift may be seen as yet another event in the Cold War which had developed between the USSR and the USA. However, it was more than that. For the first time, the former **Allies** came close to fighting each other. The consequences of the airlift were enormous.

1 GERMANY WAS SPLIT

Any hope of reuniting Germany was now ended. In May 1949, the western Allies brought their zones together to form the Federal Republic of Germany, known as West Germany. In October, the eastern sector became a separate state, calling itself the German Democratic Republic (East Germany). It had become impossible to have a peace treaty with the whole of Germany – and there never was one. Berlin, too, was more clearly divided than in the past. The British, Americans and French built up West Berlin to show the East Germans what capitalism could achieve. Meanwhile, the USSR encouraged East Berliners to think of themselves as part of East Germany and the communist system there.

2 NATO

Even before the Berlin Airlift, some western countries had talked of setting up a defensive organisation to protect themselves from the USSR. In April 1949, 12 western nations signed a treaty setting up the North Atlantic Treaty Organisation (NATO). They agreed that, if one member was attacked, others would come to its aid.

President Truman said it was 'a shield against aggression' but, at first, NATO was no match for the USSR if there had been a war. Four months after it was formed, the USSR exploded its first atomic bomb. By 1950, NATO had just 14 army divisions; the USSR and her allies could muster 173. NATO only developed as a major military force during the 1950s.

The USSR condemned NATO. It said NATO was not defensive, but an offensive alliance against the USSR. It claimed that the west was preparing for war. Soviet opposition increased when Turkey and Greece joined NATO in 1951.

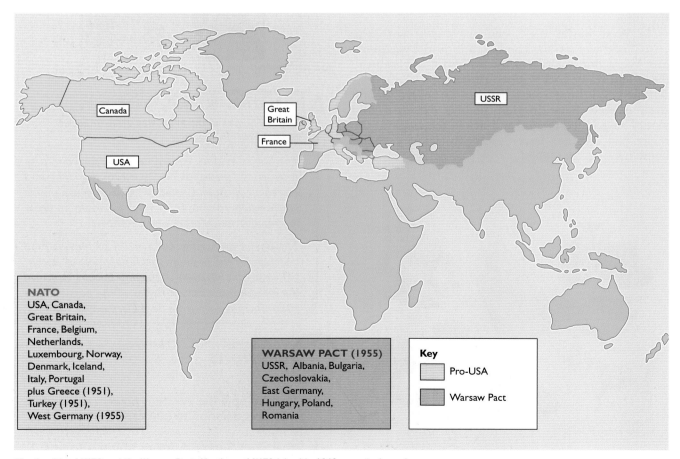

NATO
USA, Canada, Great Britain, France, Belgium, Netherlands, Luxembourg, Norway, Denmark, Iceland, Italy, Portugal plus Greece (1951), Turkey (1951), West Germany (1955)

WARSAW PACT (1955)
USSR, Albania, Bulgaria, Czechoslovakia, East Germany, Hungary, Poland, Romania

Key
Pro-USA
Warsaw Pact

Membership of NATO and the Warsaw Pact. Members of NATO joined in 1949, except where shown.

3 THE WARSAW PACT

In 1951, Greece and Turkey joined NATO. In 1955, West Germany also joined.

In 1955, the USSR set up the **Warsaw Pact**. All the countries of eastern Europe except Yugoslavia joined. They agreed to help each other if they were attacked. Each country let Stalin station Russian troops there, and put its armies under Russian generals controlled from Moscow.

1945	USA – A-BOMB
1949	RUSSIA – A-BOMB
1952	BRITAIN – A-BOMB
1952	USA – H-BOMB
1953	USSR – H-BOMB
1957	BRITAIN – H-BOMB
1957	USSR – INTERCONTINENTAL BALLISTIC MISSILE (ICBM)
1960	FRANCE – A-BOMB

Milestones in the Arms Race.

4 THE ARMS RACE

After 1949, both sides feared the other. And because they felt they were in danger, both sides built up their armies and weapons. The result, however, was that both sides felt even *more* threatened, and they built up their armed forces even more. During the 1950s, America doubled its air force and increased its army to 3.5 million men. By the 1960s, the Warsaw Pact had 4 million soldiers.

What made this so very dangerous was that both sides had nuclear weapons – in the 1950s, both sides developed the hydrogen bomb, which could wipe out a city with a single bomb. By the mid-1950s, American B52 bombers based in Europe could destroy Moscow. By the end of the 1950s, it was estimated that if the Russians attacked America, 20 million Americans would die.

Question

Which was more important as a reason for the development of the Cold War in the years 1945–9:
• The Soviet take-over of eastern Europe; or
• The Berlin Blockade 1948–9?
You must refer to both reasons when explaining your answer. [10 marks]

1. Write notes to tell the story of the Berlin Blockade, June 1948 to May 1949.
2. Write a paragraph of notes on each of the following:
• 'The division of Germany'
• 'NATO'
• 'The Warsaw Pact'
• 'The Arms Race'.

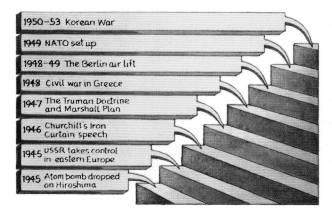

1950–53 Korean War
1949 NATO set up
1948–49 The Berlin air lift
1948 Civil war in Greece
1947 The Truman Doctrine and Marshall Plan
1946 Churchill's Iron Curtain speech
1945 USSR takes control in eastern Europe
1945 Atom bomb dropped on Hiroshima

Steps in the Cold War.

Controversy!
'The Arms Race was a ridiculous waste of time, money and energy assembling an arsenal that neither side had any intention of ever using. Both sides built up far too many weapons – all that was needed was one or two atomic bombs aimed at the other's capital city. The "Arms Race" was simply a ruse by American arms manufacturers to keep on making money.'
What is your INSTANT REACTION?

6 PEACEFUL COEXISTENCE

Key Issue

How secure was the USSR's control over eastern Europe?

AFTER STALIN

Stalin died in 1953 and the Cold War thawed a little. After a power struggle, Nikita Khrushchev emerged as the new Soviet leader. In 1955, he met western leaders at a **summit meeting** in Geneva. They agreed that Austria should now become an independent state. (They had jointly occupied it since 1945.)

In the following year, Khrushchev called for 'peaceful coexistence' with the USA. What he meant was that the two **superpowers** would have to learn to live peacefully with each other. This helped to begin a process called 'détente' in which tension between the two superpowers eased, leading to better relations. This policy of moving away from Stalin's harsh and confrontational policies is called **de-Stalinisation**. However, the process of détente regularly suffered setbacks, during which relations became tense again.

There were good reasons for following a policy of peaceful coexistence. As Khrushchev said in 1959: 'There are two ways: either peaceful coexistence or the most destructive war in history. There is no third way.' By 1960, each superpower already had enough nuclear weapons to destroy the other several times over. Khrushchev appreciated how stupid, as well as dangerous, the situation had become (see Source A). Neither side gained anything by increasing tension. There was a risk it might lead to a nuclear war which nobody wanted. Also, if the USA and USSR could agree on arms cuts, it would save money.

ARMS RACE

Yet the build-up of arms went on. In 1953, the USSR successfully tested its own H-bomb. In 1957, it produced an inter-continental ballistic missile (**ICBM**), just months before the USA produced its own ICBM. That same year, the USSR launched the first space satellite, Sputnik 1.

Another summit meeting was planned for May 1960 but, on 1 May, the Russians shot down an American plane which had been flying over the USSR. It was a U-2 spy plane, designed to take photographs of Soviet military targets. These flights had been going on for three years. When President Eisenhower refused to apologise, the meeting collapsed. It had lasted just three hours. Overhead, a Soviet sputnik circled the globe twice.

The arms race continued into the 1960s as each superpower built more nuclear weapons and also developed new ones. In 1963, both the USA and the USSR produced their first nuclear submarines.

One key reason for this was money. Nuclear missiles were cheaper to make than many conventional weapons. Also, having nuclear weapons meant that the USA did not need a large army. It seemed as if building nuclear weapons saved money, but ordinary people in many nations were frightened of them.

THE TWENTIETH PARTY CONGRESS (1956)

In February 1956, Khrushchev made a secret speech at the Twentieth **Party Congress** in Moscow. He attacked Stalin, blaming him for much that had happened in the USSR before the war. Khrushchev told senior party officials that Stalin had been a ruthless, brutal dictator.

Most of the major communist leaders in eastern Europe owed their jobs to Stalin's support. People in these countries angrily discussed the 'secret' speech and attacked Stalinist leaders. In June 1956, there were strikes and riots at Poznan in Poland: 53 workers were killed. A popular leader, Gomulka, was brought back to carry out reforms.

In Hungary, it was far worse – there was open revolt. The Hungarians had resented Soviet control of their country ever since it became communist in 1948. Hungary was a religious nation but its Catholic schools had been **nationalised** and religion was frowned upon. Schoolchildren were forced to learn communist history. In addition, the secret police (the AVO) were feared and Soviet troops still remained in the country.

Khrushchev's speech made the Hungarians feel they now had a chance to get rid of their own Stalinist leaders. At first, they were successful. The USSR forced the local communist leader, Rákosi, to resign in July 1956. But the Hungarian people were still dissatisfied: the harvest was poor and fuel was in short supply.

THE HUNGARIAN UPRISING (1956)

On 23 October, students and workers in Budapest, the capital of Hungary, held a demonstration. The Communist Party leader rejected their demands and police fired into the crowd. What had begun peacefully quickly turned into a rebellion.

A huge statue of Stalin was pulled down and dragged round the streets on a rubbish cart. Secret police were lynched and communist leaders were hanged from the trees. To calm things down, Soviet troops began withdrawing from Hungary and a moderate communist, called Imre Nagy, came to power. (It is pronounced 'Nodj'.)

The Budapest statue of Stalin was destroyed.

Nagy brought non-communists into his government and released a leading Catholic called Cardinal Mindszenty. But the situation was going beyond Nagy's control. Communists and anti-communists had joined forces. Communists wanted to end Stalinist rule; anti-communists wanted to get rid of the communists altogether. The Communist Party itself began to fall apart. Its newspaper was not published.

On 30 October, Nagy accepted all the rebels' demands. On the following day, he asked the USSR to take its troops out of Hungary. On 1 November, he announced that Hungary would leave the Warsaw Pact and become neutral. He appealed to the United Nations and asked for western help in defending the country.

Khrushchev could not tolerate this. On 4 November, Soviet tanks moved into Budapest to put down the uprising. The Hungarian people fought back with home-made weapons, such as petrol bombs, but it was a one-sided fight. About 3000–4000 Hungarians were killed and another 150,000 fled abroad. Nagy took refuge in the Yugoslav Embassy. Later in November, he was tricked out and arrested. He was executed in 1958. Cardinal Mindszenty was forced to spend the next 15 years hiding in the US Embassy before he was allowed to leave Hungary.

Nagy was replaced by the pro-Soviet Janos Kádár. He later carried out many of the reforms which Nagy had suggested. However, Hungary did not leave the Warsaw Pact. Nor did it become neutral.

Khrushchev's process of de-Stalinisation went slower after 1956 but he had shown that, in one respect, he differed little from Stalin. He had shown that eastern Europe was firmly under Soviet control and was going to stay that way.

A SOURCE

Nikita Khrushchev, quoted in *Overkill: The Story of Modern Weapons*, J Cox (1981).

President Kennedy once stated that the United States had the [missiles] to wipe out the Soviet Union two times over, while the Soviet Union had enough atomic weapons to wipe out the United States only once. Journalists asked me to comment. I said jokingly, 'He's quite right. But I'm not complaining. Once is quite enough. What good does it do to [destroy] a country twice? We're not a bloodthirsty people.'

B SOURCE

Radio Kossuth, a Hungarian radio station, 24 October 1956.

Fascist reactionary elements have started an armed attack against our public buildings and have also attacked our police. In the interest of restoring order, and until further notice is given, we announce that it is forbidden to hold any meetings, rallies and parades.

C SOURCE

Hungarian news report, 4 November 1956.

People are jumping up at the tanks, throwing hand grenades inside and then slamming the driver's windows. The Hungarian people are not afraid of death. It is only a pity that we can't stand for long.

Questions

a Study Source C. Explain the point the writer was making. Support your answer by referring to details in the source and your own knowledge. [6 marks]

b Explain why the people of Hungary rebelled against their government in 1956. [9 marks]

Key Issue

Why was Berlin once again the focus of the Cold War?

EAST BERLIN

After the Hungarian Revolution of 1956, the USSR faced less open opposition in Europe, although many eastern Europeans did not want to live behind the Iron Curtain. However, there was one place where they could leave, and that was through East Berlin.

East Berlin was a problem for the USSR. In 1953, building workers had gone on strike when the communist government increased the work they had to do by 10 per cent. As the strike spread, people demonstrated not only against their communist government but also against the USSR.

These demonstrations spread to East Germany and the police could not control them. After two days, Soviet tanks moved onto the streets of Berlin and ended the disturbances. Crowds shouted, 'Ivan, go home'.

The revolt was over but the problem of East Berlin did not go away. It was the one place in eastern Europe where people in communist countries had easy contact with people in the West. East Berliners could see the living standards of West Berliners; they could see what was on sale in the shops – and they were envious.

EAST BERLIN EXODUS

Ever since the Berlin Airlift, people had been leaving East Germany to live in the west. The total East German population was about 20 million; from 1949 onwards, over 2000 of them were leaving every day.

Communist soldiers patrolled the border between East and West Germany to stop people leaving. However, in Berlin, it was easy to get to the West. Every day, Berliners crossed the city to go to work or visit relatives. Many simply never returned.

Khrushchev wanted to solve this problem with a German peace treaty. In 1958, he demanded that all

This East Berlin frontier guard leaps to freedom in West Berlin, August 1961.

foreign troops should be pulled out of Berlin. The West believed this was part of a plan to make West Berlin part of East Germany – and therefore communist. They refused to agree.

Meanwhile, in Berlin, the refugees increased. In 1960, 199,000 East Germans left their country to live in the West. In the first six months of 1961, another 103,000 left. In August, over 3000 refugees a day were reaching West Berlin.

It was bad for communist propaganda that so many people seemed to prefer capitalism to communism. Even worse, East Germany could not afford to lose all these people, especially as many of them were skilled workers.

Khrushchev had hoped to reach an agreement over Berlin at the 1960 **summit meeting**. When talks collapsed, the USSR looked for a different solution to the problem of East Berlin.

THE BERLIN WALL (1961)

Just after midnight on 13 August 1961, the East German government took action. Police sealed off most of the crossing points in Berlin with a barrier of barbed wire. On 17 August, communist troops began to build a wall of concrete blocks. Anyone trying to escape was shot. Four died in the first two months.

Western leaders protested but there was little they could do. Extra American troops and British tanks were sent to West Berlin – but the wall stayed. To the outside world, it looked as if the USSR had won.

Churchill's 'Iron Curtain' had become real. In later years, West Berlin became a symbol of the resistance to the spread of communist oppression.

President Kennedy visited it in 1963. His eloquent speech there gave hope to those trapped on the communist side of the Wall (see Source A).

The West Berlin crowd went wild. On the other side of the wall, East Germans cheered and someone threw a bouquet over the wall.

A SOURCE

In 1963, President Kennedy told West Berliners.

There are many people in the world who really don't understand what is the great issue between the free world and the communist world.

Let them come to Berlin!

There are some who say in Europe and elsewhere we can work with the communists.

Let them come to Berlin!

All free men, wherever they may live, are citizens of Berlin. Therefore, as a free man, I take pride in the words 'Ich bin ein Berliner' [I am a Berliner].

B SOURCE

An American cartoon of the time: 'See how many are staying on our side'.

Explain how the following affected relations between the USA and USSR. Write a few sentences under each of the following headings:
● The 20th Party Congress, 1956
● The Hungarian Uprising
● Peaceful coexistence
● The Berlin Wall.

8 CZECHOSLOVAKIA (1968)

Key Issue

- Why did the USSR invade Czechoslovakia?

ANTI-SOVIET FEELINGS

In 1956, Soviet tanks had crushed the uprising in Hungary. This action showed that the USSR would not tolerate countries in eastern Europe who wanted to go their own way. It was 1968 before another communist country tried to win some independence from the USSR. This time, it was Czechoslovakia.

Czechoslovakia had been a democratic country before World War II. Its standard of living had been high. Even under communist control, it was more industrialised than most of the **satellite** states. However, its economic achievements were not as great as its people hoped.

The country was suffering from severe **inflation** and people complained that it was being exploited by the Soviet Union. There were student protests and criticism of the Czech Communist Party.

In January 1968, a new man was chosen as First Secretary of the Communist Party. His name was Alexander Dubcek. He wanted to improve the economy. He planned to do this by having less central planning, with more privately owned businesses. People would be able to travel to the West and the Communist Party would change, allowing criticisms of its methods and policies. There would be new freedoms for the people:

- freedom of assembly, allowing people to organise meetings and political parties;
- freedom of religion;
- political prisoners freed;
- trade unions allowed;
- limits on the powers of the security police;
- press censorship to end; and
- a new National Assembly would be elected, in which communists would not have all the power.

These changes would make Czechoslovakia very different to other communist nations, so Dubcek tried to reassure the USSR. He told them that Czechoslovakia would not leave the Warsaw Pact.

THE PRAGUE SPRING

Dubcek called his plans 'socialism with a human face'. This meant that his style of socialism would also allow freedom for the people. The Czechoslovak people discussed politics openly for the first time in years. People called it 'the Prague Spring': it was as if the nation were being reborn.

The Czech people supported Dubcek's reforms, as did Yugoslavia and Romania, but the USSR did not. Soviet leaders tried to persuade Dubcek to give up his reforms. They were afraid that Czechoslovakia might leave the Warsaw Pact, whatever Dubcek said. They were also worried about the effect his changes might have on other communist countries.

The Prague Spring gave way to early summer. Soviet politicians continued to talk to Dubcek. Meanwhile, behind the scenes, they planned to invade Czechoslovakia, just as they had invaded Hungary in 1956. In early May, Soviet tanks began moving through Poland and East Germany towards Czechoslovakia. By late July, about 75,000 Soviet troops were in position just outside the Czechoslovakian border.

In July, the USSR and four other Warsaw Pact countries sent a message to Dubcek. In effect, they asked him to change his policy. He did not. Dubcek did not believe the USSR would invade Czechoslovakia; nor did Tito, the Yugoslav president, who visited the country in August.

According to the USSR, what happened next was that they received a letter from leading Czech communists. It asked for Soviet help in putting down a **counter-revolution**. (No one is sure whether this is true or whether the letter was made up.)

On the night of 20–21 August 1968, Soviet troops entered Czechoslovakia. There were also a few troops from Poland, Bulgaria, Hungary and East Germany to make it look like a Warsaw Pact joint exercise.

Czech students burning Communist Party newspapers in August 1968.

One Czech official who saw them thought they were shooting a film: he did not believe his country was being invaded. Most Czechs did not resist because they knew there was no point: they could not hope to win. Faced with Soviet rifles, they placed flowers in the barrels.

However, some fought back. Barricades were set up in the streets and tanks were blown up. Students tore down street names to confuse the invaders. Anti-Soviet broadcasters stayed on the air by moving from one hiding place to another.

Meanwhile, Dubcek had been arrested and taken to Moscow where he was forced to sign an agreement, ending most of his reforms. The official Soviet version of the invasion bore no relation to the truth (see Source D). He returned to Czechoslovakia but could not bring the Czech resistance under control. In April 1969, he was forced out of office and a pro-Soviet leader called Gustav Husák took over. He clamped down on all opposition inside the country.

A SOURCE

April 1968: Svoboda, the Czech president (holding a hat) stands beside Alexander Dubcek (to his right) outside the cathedral in Prague.

B SOURCE

Dubcek described his thoughts at this moment in *Hope Dies Last* (1993).

I thought that we could [win] against the Soviets because in the end their bullying would not exceed certain limits. The 1956 crushing of Hungary was way behind us: they would not repeat that. Most of the world agreed.

C SOURCE

Spot the difference. This photograph was used in Czechoslovakia after 1969. Compare it with Source A.

D SOURCE

The official Soviet version was given by Tass, the Soviet news agency, 21 August 1968.

Party and government leaders of the Czechoslovak Socialist Republic have asked the Soviet Union and other states to give brotherly help to the Czechoslovak people with armed forces. This request was brought about by the threat from counter-revolutionary forces. The troops will be withdrawn as soon as the threat to Czechoslovakia and neighbouring communist countries has been eliminated.

Questions

a **What was the Prague Spring? [6 marks]**
b **What does Source C tell us about Czechoslovakia after Dubcek's removal? [3 marks]**
c **How reliable is Source C to an historian studying the methods of communist governments? Use Source C and your own knowledge to explain your answer. [6 marks]**

CONTAINMENT

In the early 1950s, many Americans believed that the USSR was trying to turn the whole world communist. This was what President Truman himself believed. So did President Eisenhower, who took over from him in 1953. As a result, Eisenhower built up American armed forces and nuclear weapons. He also followed Truman's policy of containment – trying to contain communism and stop it spreading.

One way of achieving this was to build up a series of alliances. NATO was the first in 1949. It was followed by SEATO (South East Asia Treaty Organisation) in 1954. The USA, Britain and France allied with five eastern countries. They agreed to act jointly should one of them be attacked. In 1955, the Baghdad Pact linked up five nations with the USA.

THE LEAD UP TO WAR

In 1949, the communists took control in China. This was a blow to the USA because Americans had been supporting Chinese Nationalists. It seemed as though the US policy of containing communism had failed in Asia. One year later, attention was focused on China's neighbour, Korea.

Korea had been ruled by Japan until Japan was defeated in the Second World War in 1945. At Yalta, Britain, the USA and USSR had agreed that Soviet and American troops should occupy Korea when the war ended. The country was divided along the 38th parallel, until a democratic government could be elected to rule the whole country. Soviet troops moved into northern Korea and American troops moved into the southern part.

The UN tried to have elections but the USSR rejected the idea. In August 1948, the Americans set up a republic in the south (the Republic of Korea). Syngman Rhee became its first president. A month later, the Russians set up a communist republic in the north (the Korean People's Democratic Republic). It was ruled by Kim Il Sung, a Red Army captain. Each claimed to represent the whole of Korea.

A portrait photograph of Kim Il Sung.

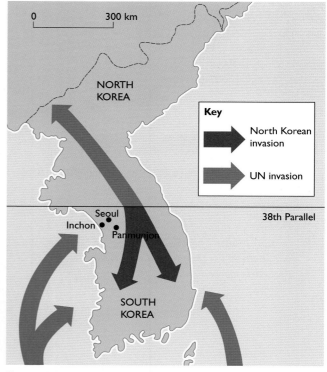

Korea and the start of war, 1950.

The United Nations believed that 18,000 people died on the border during the next two years of 'peace'. After the USA and USSR withdrew their troops, the two Korean governments continued arguing.

At dawn on 25 June 1950, these arguments led to war when North Korean troops launched a huge surprise attack on the South. The army had been equipped and trained by the USSR. Within three days, it had captured South Korea's capital, Seoul.

THE UN IS INVOLVED

The Americans acted quickly. President Truman sent supplies to the South Koreans and battleships to wait off the coast. He also asked the UN Security Council to take action. This was the first major test for the United Nations which had been formed only five years earlier. Would it take action?

When the Security Council met to discuss Korea, the USSR's representative was absent. The USSR had walked out of the UN as a protest because communist China was excluded. The Soviet Union would probably have used its veto to stop UN involvement – but it was not there to do so.

The Security Council passed a resolution, asking North Korea to leave South Korea. The North Koreans ignored this. So, days later, it passed a second resolution. This one asked UN members to send troops to help South Korea.

About 20 of the UN's 60 members eventually provided men and equipment, but it was mainly an American force. About half of the soldiers were American and the USA provided nearly all of the navy and air force. The force was led by an American, General Douglas MacArthur. He took his orders from the American president, not from the UN.

By August 1950, North Korean troops occupied nearly all of South Korea. In September, American and South Korean troops landed at Inchon, 200 miles behind the North Korean front line. The North Koreans realised they might be surrounded and quickly retreated.

However, the Americans did not stop when they had pushed the North Koreans back to the 38th parallel. General MacArthur, leading the UN troops, invaded North Korea and by October had reached the Yalu River on the Chinese frontier. This worried the Chinese who were afraid that their new communist state would be attacked.

A SOURCE

A British cartoon at the start of the war. It shows the US president, Harry Truman, with the United Nations, rushing to the aid of South Korea.

B SOURCE

Nikita Khrushchev (later Soviet leader) (from *Khrushchev Remembers*, 1971).

At the end of 1949, Kim Il Sung arrived to hold consultations with Stalin. The North Koreans wanted to prod South Korea with the point of a bayonet. Kim Il Sung said that the first poke would touch off an explosion in South Korea and that [they would turn communist].

Stalin persuaded Kim Il Sung that he should think it over, make some calculations, and then come back with a concrete plan. Kim went home and then returned to Moscow when he had worked everything out. He told Stalin he was certain of success. I remember Stalin had his doubts. He was worried that the Americans would jump in but we were inclined to think that if the war were fought swiftly, then intervention by the USA could be avoided.

Nevertheless, Stalin decided to ask Mao Zedong's opinion. [Mao Zedong was the Chinese leader.] I must stress that the war wasn't Stalin's idea, but Kim Il Sung's. Stalin, of course, didn't try to [stop] him.

Questions

a Describe the events which led to the outbreak of the Korean War. [6 marks]
b What point is the cartoonist making about the difference between the United Nations and the League of Nations in Source A? [3 marks]
c How reliable is Source A to an historian studying the outbreak of the Korean War? Use Source A and your own knowledge to answer the question. [6 marks]

CHINA JOINS IN

Before the war began, a number of countries had recognised the new People's Republic of China. This meant that they accepted that it was an independent nation. They included Britain. However, the USA refused to recognise communist China, so the Chinese were wary of the Americans.

At first, the Chinese were worried that the USA might use atomic bombs against them. But western spies told Chinese leaders that President Truman would not agree to use them. So, when the USA ignored Chinese warnings, the Chinese launched a surprise attack across the Korean border.

The Chinese army numbered 180,000 men, with another 100,000 in reserve: it was too big for the UN force to cope with. Within a fortnight, UN troops were pushed back into South Korea.

The UN force managed to halt the Chinese advance in late January. Two months later, the Chinese were pushed back across the 38th parallel into North Korea. MacArthur wanted to attack China itself. Many Americans wanted President Truman to use atomic bombs against the Chinese but he refused – though he did consider it (see Source A). MacArthur was sacked when he, too, advised the use of atom bombs.

STALEMATE

For nearly a year, the war had see-sawed back and forth across Korea. Now, it settled into a stalemate. The two sides dug trenches and faced each other across the 38th parallel. But the fighting went on. Peace talks were held at Panmunjom, on the border between the two Koreas, but dragged on for two years. While the USA and China argued, the death toll rose.

THE END OF THE WAR

In November 1952, General Eisenhower was elected as the new US President after promising to end the Korean War. He also threatened to bomb the Chinese with America's new hydrogen bomb. Then, in March 1953, Stalin died and the USSR stopped supplying weapons to the Chinese.

Soon afterwards, the Chinese agreed to talks and an **armistice** was signed at Panmunjom on 27 July 1953. The two sides agreed to fix the border close to the 38th parallel, where it had been before the war.

THE WAR'S RESULTS

It was a costly war. As many as four million people may have died. They included 54,000 Americans and about 7000 from the **British Commonwealth**. Whole areas of Korea had been destroyed; they included millions of homes.

The war led to an increase in the arms race. The USA developed a hydrogen bomb in 1952; a year later, the USSR tested one. In the 1960s, the Chinese developed both atomic and hydrogen bombs.

The war had been a testing-ground for other weapons. US troops used flame-throwers to destroy undergrowth in which enemy troops could hide. US planes dropped napalm: it burns trees and bushes easily; it also sticks to human beings and burns their flesh. Both these weapons would be used again in the Vietnam War.

It was an important war for the United Nations. The League of Nations had failed to stop aggression

This Soviet cartoon accused Trygve Lie, the UN Secretary General, of allowing UN troops to use germ warfare in Korea (1952).

in the 1930s. The UN had proved that it could raise an army and that it was prepared to stand up to aggression. Without the UN action, it is unlikely that South Korea would still exist.

In August 1950, the USSR again took its seat in the Security Council to make sure the UN could not take more steps without its agreement. It was soon using its veto again. But Stalin blamed the UN Secretary General, Trygve Lie, for getting the UN involved in Korea. Soviet representatives at the UN refused to work with him, which made his position almost impossible. In 1953, he resigned.

The Korean War, 1950–1.

But the UN failed to bring **democracy** to Korea. Kim ruled the North as a dictator until his death in 1994. Syngman Rhee was forced out of office in 1960 after complaints about government corruption. Neither North nor South has had a good record on human rights.

Above all, the UN failed to unite Korea. The border remains on the 38th parallel and all efforts to unite the country have failed. Both North and South still claim the right to rule the whole of Korea.

WAS WW III A REAL RISK?

It had been a very dangerous war indeed. During the war, the USSR had an airforce division based in northern China and support troops in North Korea. These included radar units and anti-aircraft guns. They were all used to fight American troops.

From 1951–3, American and Soviet planes fought each other over Korea. Soviet pilots wore Chinese uniforms and put Chinese symbols on their planes. In effect, Stalin had ordered Soviet troops to fight American ones. American leaders knew what was happening but kept it secret. If the American people had learned about it, they would have wanted a direct attack on the USSR.

The USA and Britain were both worried that the USSR might test the western powers elsewhere. Western leaders believed that there was a greater risk of a world war because of Korea. The war convinced the West that Stalin would do anything to expand Soviet power.

They had good reason to be concerned. Stalin had greater control over the war than western intelligence knew at the time. At one point, Stalin even considered whether to use Soviet troops to attack UN troops in Korea (see Source B). The Chinese were in agreement (see Source C).

A SOURCE

President Truman considered a direct attack on the USSR. He wrote the following in his diary in January 1952.

It seems to me that the proper approach now would be an ultimatum [to] Moscow. This means all-out war. Every manufacturing plant in China and the Soviet Union will be eliminated. This is the final chance for the Soviet government to decide whether it wishes to survive or not.

B SOURCE

Stalin considered war with the USA. He sent this telegram to Mao Zedong in October 1950.

Should we fear this? I think not, because together we shall be stronger than America, England and the other capitalist states. Without Germany, they do not represent a serious military power. If war is inevitable, then let it be now.

C SOURCE

Mao Zedong replied in October 1950.

I am very happy that in your reply the joint struggle of the USSR and China against the Americans is discussed. Undoubtedly, if we are to fight, then we should fight now.

Question

Which was more responsible as a reason for the development of the Cold War in the years 1945–53:
- **The Soviet take-over of eastern Europe; or**
- **The Korean War, 1950–3?**

You must refer to both reasons when explaining your answer. [10 marks]

Explain the causes, course and results of the Korean War. Write a few sentences under the following headings:
- The lead up to the Korean War
- The role of the UN
- Chinese intervention
- Consequences of the war.

Key Issue

How close did the world come to a Third World War?

By 1960, the two superpowers had enough nuclear missiles to wipe out each other and everyone else as well. However, they were still nervous. What would happen if their missiles were destroyed before they could use them? Or suppose they were destroyed in mid-flight? Both the USA and USSR became worried that nuclear missiles alone did not offer a final solution.

So each side developed its own nuclear deterrents. These would deter the enemy from using its missiles. This would be achieved by making sure that your own side could still strike back even after being attacked by nuclear weapons – resulting in both sides being wiped out. This theory was known as **MAD** (Mutually Assured Destruction).

BACKGROUND

The island of Cuba lies about 90 miles off the United States coast. From 1952 to 1959, it was ruled by a dictator called General Batista. The USA supported him for most of that time. American companies controlled much of Cuban business. As long as Cuba was at peace, American business profited. So the USA supplied Batista with arms.

However, Batista's rule became more and more brutal and, in 1957, the USA cut off arms supplies. It wanted a more effective government so it encouraged a resistance movement, led by Fidel Castro. In 1959, he overthrew Batista's government and became Cuban President. By then, he had become communist.

The friendly relations between Castro and the USA did not last for long. Castro began a series of reforms, which included nationalising some Cuban industries. Many of these were American.

Also, Castro blamed the USA for the island's poverty and sought aid from the USSR. When the USA refused to buy Cuba's sugar, the USSR agreed to take the sugar in return for oil and machinery.

THE BAY OF PIGS (1961)

President Eisenhower promised to help Cuban refugees who wanted to get rid of Castro. In January 1961, John F Kennedy took over as US President, the youngest in the country's history. He was told of a **CIA** plan to invade Cuba and overthrow Castro. He allowed the plan to go ahead and the result was a disaster.

On 17 April, about 1500 of Castro's opponents landed at Cochinos Bay ('the Bay of Pigs') on the southern coast of Cuba. They were equipped with arms provided by the USA. These rebels had told the CIA that the Cubans would join them and overthrow Castro; they did not.

The group was badly trained and poorly armed and equipped. Even their maps were out-of-date. In any case, they were outnumbered by almost 300 to one. Within three days, the invaders were either dead or in prison. Kennedy was furious with the CIA for recommending the invasion (see Source A).

The results of this invasion were the opposite to what the CIA intended. First, the Cuban army had defeated the invaders so easily that Castro became more popular. Secondly, Castro now saw the USA as a very serious threat indeed. He asked Khrushchev for help to defend Cuba.

This invader (the one with his hands up) was captured two days after the Bay of Pigs invasion.

MISSILE SITES

Throughout 1962, American intelligence kept watch over Cuba. In the summer, CIA agents reported that Soviet ships were seen heading for the island. Down at the docks, Cubans were thrown out of their homes while Soviet sentries guarded ships which were being unloaded.

In September, the USSR admitted supplying arms to Castro but said they were for Cuban defence only. This seemed to make sense: if the USSR wished to attack the USA with nuclear weapons, it did not need to go to Cuba to do it. It could have launched them from bases within the USSR.

On 16 October 1962, Kennedy received evidence which suggested that Khrushchev had lied. An American U-2 spy plane had flown over Cuba and taken photographs. These pictures showed that rocket-launching sites were being built on the island. From these sites the Cubans would be able to fire atomic missiles at almost any major American city.

WHAT SHOULD KENNEDY DO?

Kennedy faced a difficult decision. The Cold War was at its height and the USSR seemed to be winning it. In 1960, the USA had been publicly humiliated when a U-2 spy plane had been shot down over the Soviet Union. In August 1961, the communists had built the Berlin Wall (see pages 16–17).

The USA had been embarrassed again in 1961 when the world learned of the Bay of Pigs fiasco. Was Khrushchev testing Kennedy's nerve, to see whether the young president would stand up to him (see Source B)? Whether he was or not, Kennedy had to decide what to do about the Cuban missiles.

These five options were considered by Kennedy's advisers:

1. Do nothing.
2. Offer to remove US missile bases in Turkey in exchange for the removal of Cuban missiles.
3. **Blockade** Cuba, e.g. by putting ships around it.
4. Launch an air attack on the missile sites.
5. Invade and occupy the entire island of Cuba.

A SOURCE

This was what Kennedy told a friend after the Bay of Pigs failure (from *Kennedy*, R Gadney, 1983).

How could I have been so far off base? All my life I've known better than to depend on the experts. How could I have been so stupid to let them go ahead?

B SOURCE

In June 1961, Kennedy and Khrushchev held a summit conference in Vienna. Khrushchev was hostile, as Kennedy told a reporter.

I've got two problems. First, to figure out why he [acted] in such a hostile way. Second, to figure out what we can do about it. I think he [was hostile] because of the Bay of Pigs. I think he thought that anyone who was so young and inexperienced as to get into a mess like that could be taken. And anyone who got into it, and didn't see it through, had no guts. So I've got a terrible problem. If he thinks I'm inexperienced and have no guts, until we remove those ideas we won't get anywhere with him.

Question

Describe the key features of the Bay of Pigs conflict in 1961. [6 marks]

This American photo showed Soviet missiles heading for Cuba (1962).

KENNEDY'S DECISION

Kennedy consulted with his advisers and decided to use the US navy to blockade Cuba. This would stop Soviet ships from landing any more missiles or other weapons. However, there was no guarantee that the USSR would tolerate this. They might take action themselves, such as seizing West Berlin.

So, in western America, 156 **ICBMs** were primed, ready to be fired at once. Meanwhile, the US air force was put on stand-by and nuclear bombs were loaded into the bomb bays (on the planes).

The outside world knew nothing of this. The first news of the crisis was given by President Kennedy himself when he appeared on television on 22 October 1962. He announced the blockade and asked Khrushchev to stop supplying missiles to Cuba. And he went further to say that the United states would:

> 'regard any nuclear missile launched from Cuba against any nation in the Western Hemisphere as an attack by the Soviet Union on the United States, requiring a full retaliatory response upon the Soviet Union.'

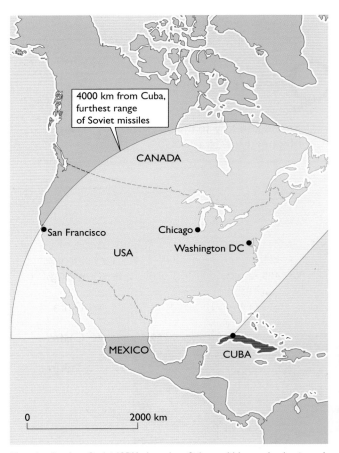

4000 km from Cuba, furthest range of Soviet missiles

CANADA

San Francisco

Chicago

Washington DC

USA

MEXICO

CUBA

0   2000 km

Map showing how Soviet ICBMs based on Cuba could have wiped out much of the United States.

THE SOVIET DECISION

Kennedy's meaning was obvious. If a Cuban missile was launched, the USA would attack the USSR. The world held its breath. On 23 October, the Soviet Press Officer at the UN told an American: 'This could well be our last conversation. New York will be blown up tomorrow by Soviet nuclear weapons. The Kremlin won't stand for this!'

In fact, he was wrong. The following day, 12 Soviet ships heading for Cuba either stopped or changed course. 'We're eyeball to eyeball,' said the US Secretary of State, 'and I think the other fellow just blinked.'

On Cuba itself, work continued on the missile sites. In the United States, Kennedy mobilised troops, ready for a possible invasion of Cuba. But the Russians were looking for a way out of the crisis. The two leaders talked by telephone and Khrushchev sent Kennedy two letters (see Sources A and B).

HOW DID IT END?

Many people believed that a nuclear war might start at any minute. On one occasion, the US navy boarded a USSR merchant ship – but the USSR did not retaliate. On another occasion, a Soviet missile shot down a U-2 plane over Cuba, killing the pilot: this time, the USA took no action.

The crisis ended on 28 October. The public was told that the USSR agreed to remove its missiles from Cuba and not install any more. In return, Kennedy ended the American blockade and also promised not to invade the island.

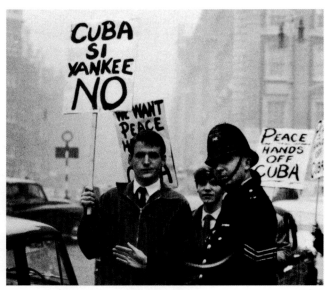

Around the world, there were demonstrations against American policy on Cuba. This one was in London.

In fact, President Kennedy had struck a secret deal with the USSR. Neither the public nor the US government was told about it. Kennedy had promised to remove some missiles from Europe if Khrushchev removed Soviet ones from Cuba. In November 1962, the Soviet missiles were dismantled. In April 1963, American Jupiter missiles were quietly withdrawn from Britain, Italy and Turkey.

RESULTS OF THE CRISIS

The two superpowers had come dangerously close to a war. Neither Kennedy nor Khrushchev wanted to run the risk of a similar clash in the future. So a direct telephone line was set up in 1963 between Moscow and Washington. The two leaders could use this 'hotline' to talk directly to each other at just a few minutes' notice.

In that same year, a Test Ban Treaty was signed by the USA, USSR and Britain. They agreed to stop all nuclear tests in the atmosphere. However, it was not signed by either France or China. The French already had an atomic bomb; China exploded its first in 1964. The USSR's leaders did not share Khrushchev's view of the Soviet 'success' (see Source D). In 1964 he was quietly removed from power by the Communist Party.

A SOURCE

This is from Khrushchev's first letter, received on 26 October 1962.

This is my proposal. No more weapons to Cuba and those within Cuba withdrawn or destroyed, and you respond by ending your blockade and also agree not to invade Cuba. Do not interfere with Russian ships.

B SOURCE

This is from Khrushchev's second letter which arrived on 27 October.

Your rockets are situated in Britain, situated in Italy and are aimed at us. Your rockets are situated in Turkey. You are worried by Cuba. You say that it worries you because it is a distance of 90 miles from America, but Turkey is next to us. Our sentries walk up and down and look at each other.

I therefore make this proposal: we agree to remove [the missiles] from Cuba; we agree to carry this out and make a pledge to the United Nations. Your representatives will [declare] that the United States will remove its [missiles] from Turkey.

C SOURCE

This British cartoon showed how serious the situation had been (November 1962). It shows Khrushchev (left) and Kennedy.

D SOURCE

Nikita Khrushchev gave his view of the crisis in his autobiography, *Khrushchev Remembers* (1971).

We had to find a way of stopping US interference in the Caribbean. The answer was missiles. I had the idea of installing missiles with nuclear warheads in Cuba without letting the United States find out they were there until it was too late to do anything about them. We had no desire to start a war.

We sent the Americans a note saying that we agreed to remove our missiles and bombers on the condition that the President [promised] that there would be no invasion of Cuba by the forces of the United States or anybody else.

Finally Kennedy gave in and agreed to [give] us such an assurance. It was a great victory for us, a spectacular success without having to fire a single shot!

Questions

a Study Source C. Explain the message of this cartoon. Support your answer by referring to details of the cartoon and your knowledge. [6 marks]
b Explain why there was a crisis over Cuba in 1962. [9 marks]
c How did the United States react to Castro's revolution in Cuba? [4 marks]
d Why was the Bay of Pigs invasion a failure? [6 marks]
e Explain how the following together contributed to the Cuban Missiles Crisis:
  • The Bay of Pigs
  • The US blockade of Cuba
  • US missiles in Turkey. [10 marks]

11 VIETNAM

Key Issue

Why did the United States get involved?

THE DOMINO THEORY

In the nineteenth century, the French had added a huge part of South East Asia to their empire. This area was known as Indo-China. During the Second World War, Japanese troops occupied the area. Local people did not want to be ruled by foreigners so they organised **resistance** groups. One of them was the Vietminh. It was a mainly communist group, led by Ho Chi Minh.

Japan surrendered on 15 August 1945; in September, Ho Chi Minh announced that Vietnam was an independent republic. The Second World War was over – but the twentieth century's longest war was about to begin.

The French wanted to keep Vietnam in their empire and French troops returned to southern Vietnam. Ho Chi Minh's Vietminh was not going to let the French re-take Vietnam without a fight. In 1946, war broke out between the French and the Vietminh.

The USA did not approve of France fighting to get its colony back. However, between 1946 and 1954, the USA gave over $1 billion to France to help them win. The USA gave all this money because they were afraid that **communism** would spread through South East Asia. This idea was known as the 'domino theory' (see Source A).

Despite all the money, the French lost. In 1953, they tried to trap the Vietminh by setting up a camp at Dien Bien Phu. The Vietminh surrounded it and set up gun positions on the nearby hills: the French could not get supplies into the camp.

From March to May 1954, the Vietminh besieged Dien Bien Phu in North Vietnam. After two months, the French were defeated and the survivors were put in prison camps. Another two months later, an **armistice** was signed and the French agreed to leave Indo-China. There had been 16,500 French troops at Dien Bien Phu; only 3000 lived to tell the story.

VIETNAM DIVIDED

The peace talks were held at Geneva. It was agreed that Vietnam would be split into two parts, along the line of the 17th parallel. The north became a communist republic, controlled by the Vietminh. In 1955, southern Vietnam, too, became a republic, with Ngo Dinh Diem as president. The plan was that an election for the whole country would be held two years later and the country would be united.

However, many of the South Vietnamese also supported Ho Chi Minh. An election would turn the whole of Vietnam into a communist country. So the USA promised to support the South Vietnamese government, despite the fact that it refused to take part in an election.

South East Asia, showing Vietnam divided.

WHY DID THE USA GET INVOLVED?

Ho Chi Minh wanted a united, communist Vietnam. The USA believed that he was being supported by the Chinese to turn the whole of South East Asia communist. President Eisenhower (1953–61) believed in the domino theory: if South Vietnam became communist, Laos and Cambodia might be the next targets.

So the USA supported Diem's government of South Vietnam, based in Saigon. It was mainly made up of rich Roman Catholic landowners. Diem's rule was harsh and his government was unpopular with the peasants, many of whom were Buddhists.

His government was also corrupt. The Americans sent money to help Diem's government; much of it was used to bribe Diem's friends. The USA sent arms, too: some were even sold to the communists.

Buddhists were persecuted by Diem's government and tried to draw the world's attention to Vietnam. This Buddhist monk chose to protest by committing suicide (1963).

1960–3

By 1960, whole areas of South Vietnam were in open rebellion. That same year, the National Liberation Front (NLF) was set up to oppose Diem; its members were mostly communist and received help from North Vietnam. The South Vietnamese government called them the Vietcong. A civil war was developing between the government and its peasant opponents.

President Kennedy (1961–3) became very concerned. American money and arms had not saved the South Vietnamese government. So he decided to send more advisers, as well. By November 1963, about 10,000 US advisers were helping South Vietnamese troops.

Meanwhile, the South Vietnamese army tortured and executed thousands of peasants in an attempt to destroy the NLF. This made the peasants even more determined to fight back. In November 1963, Diem's hated government was overthrown and Diem was killed. Outside the palace in Saigon, crowds celebrated.

FULL-SCALE US WAR

Later that month, Kennedy himself was assassinated. The new president was Lyndon Johnson. He decided to increase American help to the South Vietnamese. The US Navy patrolled the Vietnamese coast on the look-out for NLF soldiers. In August 1964, the North Vietnamese retaliated and attacked an American destroyer in the Gulf of Tonkin.

THE TONKIN RESOLUTION (1964)

Johnson already had secret plans to escalate the war but could not carry them out unless he could show there was a reason to do so. The Tonkin incident gave him the excuse he needed. The US Congress passed a resolution which allowed Johnson to fight a war against the North Vietnamese. It was a decision which many Americans would later regret.

The Tonkin Resolution opened the floodgates for US involvement in Vietnam. It allowed President Johnson to use US troops to defend any SEATO country (see Source B). It allowed US aircraft to bomb North Vietnamese naval bases and oil refineries; Johnson believed it allowed him to fight a full-scale war in Vietnam and that is what he did.

The first US marines arrived in South Vietnam early in 1965; by the end of the year, there were 150,000 US troops in the country. By 1969, the number had risen to half a million.

A SOURCE

The domino theory: what the USA feared would happen in South East Asia.

B SOURCE

President Johnson, speaking in 1965.

Most of the non-communist nations of Asia cannot, by themselves, resist the growing might and ambition of Asian communism. If we are driven from the field in Vietnam, then no nation can ever again have the same confidence in American promises or American protection. In each land the forces of independence would be weakened. An Asia so threatened by communist domination would [endanger] the security of the United States itself.

Question

Which was more important as a reason for the development of the Cold War in the years 1965–73:
- **The war in Vietnam; or**
- **Events in Czechoslovakia in 1968?**

You must refer to both reasons when explaining your answer. [10 marks]

AMERICAN TACTIC: BOMBS

Johnson believed that he had to stop the North Vietnamese supplying weapons to the NLF. Therefore, the US air force bombed strategic targets in North Vietnam. They included army bases, factories, railways and bridges. By early 1966, US planes were flying an average of 164 flying missions a day. The bombs often missed their target: school children and hospital patients were among those killed.

AMERICAN TACTIC: STRATEGIC HAMLETS

The second strategy had been introduced by President Kennedy. The USA knew that the NLF was supported by most of South Vietnam's peasants. Advisers believed the USA had a better chance of winning if they could stop the peasants from keeping in touch with the NLF.

So US troops turned the peasants out of their own villages and put them in 'strategic hamlets'. These were areas surrounded by barbed wire and controlled by the Americans. About 40 per cent of the Vietnamese population was moved in this way. The scheme made the Vietnamese hate the Americans even more.

US marines in Vietnam.

NLF TACTIC: GUERRILLA WARFARE

The USA believed it could win because it had the most modern fighting equipment. The NLF had no aircraft, no tanks and no artillery. What they had instead was experience in fighting a **guerrilla war** against the French from 1946–54. They used the same tactics against the Americans.

The NLF avoided fighting the US troops in open battle because the Americans were better armed. Instead, they hid in the jungle or mingled with peasants in the rice-fields.

It was impossible for American troops to know who was a guerrilla and who was not. The NLF wore no uniform so they looked just like the peasants; they spoke the same language so they sounded just like peasants. Indeed, many of them had been peasants so they knew every detail of the jungle.

NLF guerrillas hid in a system of tunnels which stretched for 200 miles under South Vietnam. They launched hit-and-run raids from one tunnel, just 20 miles from Saigon. There was even an underground hospital system. The doctor in charge amputated limbs without anaesthetics and carried out brain surgery with an electric drill.

AMERICAN TACTIC: CHEMICALS

Both the USSR and China supplied money and weapons to the NLF. The North Vietnamese brought these weapons through the jungle at night on foot or by bicycle. The most famous route was nicknamed the Ho Chi Minh Trail. One problem for the Americans was that they could not see the people supplying the NLF because the jungle was too dense.

So the Americans dropped chemical bombs to destroy the trees. The result was defoliation – the leaves were stripped from the trees, thus allowing US helicopters to spot the enemy more easily. Napalm was also used in fire bombs and flame-throwers. It is a thick liquid, which usually contains petrol. It cleared the undergrowth but it also stuck to human beings and burned away their flesh. Ho Chi Minh reminded Johnson of America's use of these rather vicious weapons (see Source A).

The Ho Chi Minh Trail.

OPPOSITION TO WAR

In South Vietnam, innocent men, women and children were burned by napalm and civilians began to doubt whether the USA was really on their side. Increasingly, South Vietnamese people saw the NLF as friends and their own government as the enemy. US troops became more and more unpopular.

Opposition also grew in the United States. At first, most protests had been from students. But a **draft law** forced young men to go and fight in Vietnam. Black Americans were against it because draft laws hit them hardest. About 12 per cent of Americans were black, but the percentage of draftees who were black was 16 per cent. Many middle-class Americans were also against the war. By 1967, the death rate had risen to 160 American deaths a week. American parents did not want their sons to die far from home in a war they did not understand.

THE TET OFFENSIVE

In January 1968, the NLF launched the Tet Offensive, capturing 75 per cent of the main towns in South Vietnam. Even the American Embassy in the capital Saigon was captured for a few hours. In the end, the Offensive failed but the campaign had two important effects.

First, it convinced the Americans that this was a war they could not win. By 1968, more Americans opposed the Vietnam War than supported it. So, second, President Johnson stopped bombing North Vietnam in return for peace talks in Paris. Nevertheless, the number of American dead passed 30,000 by the end of the year.

This Vietnamese woman is touching the remains of her husband, killed during the Tet Offensive (1968).

A SOURCE

Ho Chi Minh wrote to President Johnson in 1967.

The US government has committed war crimes, crimes against peace and against mankind. Half a million US troops have [used] the most inhuman weapons and the most barbarous methods of warfare, such as napalm, chemicals and gases, to massacre our [countrymen], destroy crops and raze villages to the ground.

B SOURCE

These children were victims of a US napalm bomb (June 1972).

Questions

a Study Source B. Explain the importance of this photograph. Support your answer by referring to details of the photograph and your own knowledge. **[6 marks]**

b Explain the reasons for America's involvement in Vietnam. **[9 marks]**

Explain US attempts to contain communism outside Europe. Write a few sentences under each of the following headings:

- The Korean War
- Castro's revolution in Cuba
- The Bay of Pigs conflict
- The Cuban Missiles Crisis
- The consequences of the Crisis
- The division of Vietnam
- Early US involvement in Vietnam.

THE END OF THE WAR

The war made President Johnson so unpopular that he decided not to stand for re-election in 1968. The following year, the new president, Richard Nixon, introduced a new policy called Vietnamisation. What this meant was that he would go on supplying arms and money to South Vietnam – but the South Vietnamese would do the fighting. As a result, many US troops were pulled out of the country. By 1971, the number had been halved.

This picture shows the execution of an NLF officer. It created a big impact in the USA in 1968.

THE HO CHI MINH TRAIL

However, Nixon did not want the communists to win so he began bombing North Vietnam once more. In 1969, he even began secretly bombing Cambodia to stop supplies being sent to the NLF down the Ho Chi Minh Trail. These bombing raids were kept secret even from the US Congress: military records showed 'nil' raids on Cambodia and bombing records were burned. In 1970 US forces invaded Cambodia for two months. In the following year, Laos also became an American target. During Christmas 1972, the US dropped 100,000 bombs on Haiphong in North Vietnam: it was the largest bombing raid in history.

'PEACE WITH HONOUR'

Nixon wanted a way out of the war but he wanted 'peace with honour'. The man who supplied it was his foreign affairs adviser, Dr Henry Kissinger. He held secret talks with the North Vietnamese, even while the bombing and fighting continued. Indeed, the bombing was partly to persuade Americans that North Vietnam was being forced to give up.

It took four years before the two sides could agree. An armistice was finally signed at Paris in January 1973 and American troops went home. Thousands of South Vietnamese went with them, including many politicians who knew they were wanted by the communists. Kissinger's reward was the 1973 Nobel Peace Prize, which he shared with a Vietnamese delegate at the peace talks.

1973–5

There had been peace talks; there had been an agreement. But there was little peace. The fighting dragged on for two more years, with the communists gradually winning. In April 1975, the NLF captured Saigon. They renamed it Ho Chi Minh City in honour of their leader who had died in 1969.

US advisers left the city in such a rush that there was no time to burn the files which listed their Vietnamese secret agents. To the outside world, it did not look like 'peace with honour'.

THE WAR'S EFFECTS

1 THE DOMINO THEORY

President Kennedy had been afraid that, if Vietnam became communist, so would the rest of South East Asia. This happened in both Laos and Cambodia. However, it did not happen in Thailand, Burma or Malaysia. The domino theory had been proved wrong.

2 VIETNAM

Vietnam was united in 1976 but the country had been destroyed by bombing. Tropical rainforest had been reduced to scrubland; large areas of farming land were little more than a wasteland.

Since the war, thousands of refugees have left Vietnam.

Vietnam's economy was also destroyed. It went from being a major rice exporter to a country that could not feed its own people. After Vietnam was invaded by the Chinese in 1979 it relied on aid from the Soviet Union. Many professional Vietnamese fled the country, looking for safety abroad. Their departure caused more damage to the country's economy.

3 THE COST

No one knows how many people died in the Vietnam War: the total Vietnamese death toll might have been two million. Nearly 58,000 US troops died and another 300,000 were wounded. The war cost the USA $120 billion. There has also been another type of cost – a psychological one to the survivors (see Source A).

When the peace talks were over, prisoners-of-war were exchanged. But 2400 US troops were still reported as missing in Vietnam. Some Americans believed that some of them were being used as slave labour, 20 years later. One French prisoner was kept like this for 12 years.

4 US BITTERNESS

The small state of North Vietnam had beaten one of the world's **superpowers**. It was a war that many Americans wished to forget. Long afterwards, many relatives of dead **GI**s still blamed the politicians for sending their sons and husbands to Vietnam in the first place. They were also bitter about the 'draft dodgers' – the well-off young men who managed to avoid going to fight. Not a single member of the US Congress lost a son in the war.

The remains of a crashed US B-52 bomber in Vietnam (1993).

HISTORIANS LOOK BACK

As more sources become available, modern historians are reaching new conclusions about the war. In 1968, people believed that the Tet Offensive was a North Vietnamese success. It convinced many Americans that they could not win the war. Today, we know that the NLF themselves thought it was a failure. They lost many of their key fighters during the campaign.

Some historians doubt whether American public opinion really had a major impact on what the government did. When the build-up of troops was slowed down in 1969, the government was more worried about the cost of the war than what Americans thought. The American public generally still thought that the country should keep fighting, as long as there was a chance of winning.

Finally, people used to think that the USA's military could not win against the NLF's guerrilla tactics. But there is evidence that the USA's position improved between 1968 and 1972. As so often in history, it is not what happened that mattered. What counted was what people *thought* was happening.

A SOURCE

From *Superpower Rivalry* by S Judges (1994).

Some 700,000 veterans, women as well as men, have suffered psychological effects: it has been shown that they are far more likely than the rest of the population to experience panic attacks, depression, drug addiction and to be divorced or unemployed.

Questions

a **What was the importance of the Tonkin resolution? [4 marks]**
b **Why did the war become unpopular in the United States? [6 marks]**
c **Explain how the following together contributed to the defeat of the USA in Vietnam:**
  • **The tactics of the NLF**
  • **The tactics of the United States**
  • **Public opinion in the United States.**
[10 marks]

12 DÉTENTE

Key Issue

- How successful were moves towards détente in the 1970s?

THE BREZHNEV DOCTRINE

Leonid Brezhnev, the Soviet leader, stated that it was the duty of any communist country to intervene with force in any other communist country which was threatened by capitalists. This applied even to independent countries. This policy became known as the Brezhnev Doctrine.

In practice, it meant that the USSR would stop any country in the Warsaw Pact which tried to go its own way. Soviet troops had succeeded in controlling Hungary in 1956. Afterwards, Hungarian living standards had gone up and its leaders seemed popular. The Czech invasion of 1968 tried to repeat this success. It seemed as if Soviet policy had changed little in 12 years: **resistance** would still be crushed.

However, the invasion of Czechoslovakia marked a turning-point in the Cold War, though few people knew it at the time. What happened in Hungary was not repeated in Czechoslovakia. The Czech people never really trusted those who replaced Dubcek. And the Brezhnev Doctrine was almost an admission that countries would only stay communist if the USSR forced them to do so.

Czech youths protesting about the invasion.

Also, the USSR's reputation among other communists was damaged by its treatment of Czechoslovakia. The Romanian leader made a speech, attacking the Soviet action. President Tito of Yugoslavia also condemned it. So did the Chinese. There was criticism from communist parties in Britain, France, Italy and Spain.

REASONS FOR DÉTENTE

The Czech crisis had occurred when East–West relations were improving. From 1964 onwards, politicians talked about détente between East and West. Détente means a relaxing of tension.

At first, it seemed as though events in Czechoslovakia would put an end to détente. Many countries felt that they needed to strengthen their defences against a possible Soviet attack. For instance, President Tito increased the Yugoslav armed forces.

However, there were good reasons why détente continued. The Cuban Missiles Crisis had shown just how dangerous a confrontation could be. Neither side wanted the next disagreement to turn into a nuclear war. Each side already had enough nuclear weapons to destroy the other. Better relations meant that fewer weapons needed to be built. This not only saved money, it allowed western and eastern leaders to portray themselves as peace-makers.

Both the USA and USSR wanted détente because each had economic problems during the 1970s. In the USA, there was rising inflation. Money spent on nuclear weapons meant there was less available to improve living conditions for poor Americans.

The USSR, too, faced problems. It was spending 20 per cent of its budget on defence. Also, its industry was very inefficient compared with American industry. Soviet industry had to improve before its leaders could raise their people's standard of living.

Test Ban Treaty (1967) Banned nuclear tests in space

Nuclear Non-Proliferation Treaty (1968) between USA and USSR (later joined by other nations) This tried to stop smaller countries making nuclear weapons

Two agreements of the 1960s.

Lastly, there were political reasons for détente. The USSR had begun to quarrel with communist China, her huge neighbour to the south. Meanwhile, the Americans had become bogged down in the Vietnam War.

So, throughout the late 1960s and 1970s, American and Soviet leaders tried hard to reduce tension. This led to better trade links between the two superpowers after 1972. In particular, the USA sold its surplus wheat cheaply to the USSR. However, the biggest benefits of détente were agreements to limit missiles.

SALT I

Richard Nixon became US President in 1969. Both he and Brezhnev wished to improve relations between the USA and the USSR. In 1969, they made the first real attempt to limit weapons when they began the Strategic Arms Limitation Talks (SALT). These talks were concerned with expensive middle-range nuclear weapons.

Meanwhile, Nixon tried to improve relations with China. In 1971, he agreed to let China join the UN. In February 1972, he visited the Chinese capital, Beijing. Soviet leaders became worried that the USA and China might ally against the USSR.

In May 1972, Nixon visited the Soviet Union. He was the first American president to go there since Roosevelt went to Yalta in 1945. In Moscow, the two **superpowers** signed the SALT I Treaty. They agreed to limit building certain missiles for five years. However, this agreement did not reduce existing stocks of weapons.

US President Nixon (left) and Brezhnev (1972).

HELSINKI AGREEMENT (1975)

This agreement was another product of détente. Both sides officially accepted the existing borders between European countries. The leaders also agreed a Declaration of Human Rights – rights which each country promised to their people. They included: freedom of speech; freedom of religion; freedom of movement; and freedom from unfair arrest.

In effect, western leaders accepted that the USSR would continue to rule over communist eastern Europe. Soviet leaders were delighted with this. In return, they made half-hearted promises about civil rights which they did not intend to keep. While the talks went on, new Soviet medium-range missiles were secretly being put in position. They were aimed at western Europe.

WAS COMMUNISM WINNING?

The mid-1970s were the high point of détente. But the USSR's real aim had not changed: it wanted to defeat capitalism and to turn the whole world communist. Soviet leaders believed they were succeeding.

The USA's defeat in Vietnam was just one sign that capitalism seemed to be losing: Cambodia and Laos, as well as Vietnam, turned communist. In Africa, too, support for communism was growing.

SALT II

Despite SALT I, the number of Soviet and American missiles increased during the 1970s. A later American President, Jimmy Carter (1977–81), wanted both sides to get rid of nuclear weapons completely and more SALT talks were held.

A new SALT agreement was signed by Presidents Carter and Brezhnev in June 1979. This limited the number of long-range missiles, especially those with multiple warheads. But, in December, Soviet troops invaded Afghanistan. The SALT talks stopped abruptly and the US Congress refused to ratify the SALT II agreement. Détente was now under threat.

Questions

a **Explain what is meant by 'détente'. [3 marks]**
b **Describe the key features of SALT I and SALT II. [5 marks]**
c **Describe the key features of the Helsinki Agreement, 1975. [5 marks]**

Explain how successful the moves towards détente were in the 1970s. Write a few sentences under each of the following headings:
- The Czech crisis
- The Cuban Missiles Crisis
- Economic problems
- Political reasons
- SALT I and II.

13 AFGHANISTAN

Key Issue

- How did Afghanistan contribute to the collapse of détente in the late 1970s and early 1980s?

THE SOVIET INVASION

The Brezhnev Doctrine was widely attacked. Yet the criticism did not stop Brezhnev using force in Afghanistan, 11 years after Czechoslovakia.

During 1979, Afghanistan became very unsettled. Muslim opposition groups attacked the new Afghan government which was both non-Muslim and pro-Soviet. The USSR looked on uneasily. It, too, had a large Muslim population in the areas nearest to Afghanistan. Soviet leaders were worried that extremist Muslim ideas might soon affect the Soviet Union itself.

What happened next was a textbook example of how the USSR dealt with difficult neighbours. On 28 December 1979, Soviet leader Brezhnev phoned US President Jimmy Carter with some news. He told him that Soviet troops had been invited into Afghanistan to protect the country from attacks.

Afghanistan and its neighbouring countries.

In fact, Soviet troops were already in Afghanistan. The airport at Kabul, Afghanistan's capital, had been captured on Christmas Eve, to allow the USSR to bring in troops and equipment. At the same time, Soviet troops had crossed the northern border into Afghanistan.

A **KGB** squad attacked the palace in Kabul and assassinated the communist president, Hafizollah Amin. On New Year's Day 1980, a new government was set up in Kabul, led by Babrak Karmal. He was a former Afghan leader who had been in exile in the USSR. A Soviet plane had flown him back specially to take over the government.

ISLAMIC REVOLT

Criticism of the invasion was worldwide. Afghanistan's Muslim neighbours, Pakistan and Iran, both objected. So did western powers. The USA **boycotted** the 1980 Olympic Games in Moscow as a protest. That same year, Ronald Reagan was elected as the next US President after demanding that the United States build more nuclear weapons.

The USSR ignored the protests and its troops stayed. By February 1980, there were 80,000 of them. However, they soon found that putting down opposition in Afghanistan wasn't as easy as in Hungary or Czechoslovakia.

Soviet troops were supposed to support the Afghan army against the Muslim groups which were anti-communist. But they faced two problems. First, the Afghan army was not as good as they had believed. Second, they faced opposition from rebel forces, called the mujaheddin.

The rebels were not just fighting to get rid of Soviet troops. They were fighting to turn Afghanistan into a Muslim country. They were well-equipped because they were given weapons by both the USA and China, who opposed the Soviet invasion.

These boys fought for the Mujaheddin rebel forces. One of them is holding an AK-47 rifle.

SOVIET WITHDRAWAL

The mujaheddin fought a **guerrilla war** against the Soviet and Afghan armies. Soviet troops controlled the towns where they were based but the mujaheddin controlled the countryside. They attacked Soviet supply routes; they shot at Soviet transport planes. Other nations increased their pressure on the Soviet Union. The USA, for instance, banned grain exports to the USSR. In 1981, the UN General Assembly asked the USSR to leave Afghanistan: the request was ignored.

In addition to this, the USSR faced problems at home. Muslim nations, which had once been friendly, turned hostile. The USSR increasingly became worried that Muslims inside the Soviet Union might revolt. In any case, the war grew unpopular as Soviet casualties increased (see Source A).

In 1985, a new Soviet leader, Mikhail Gorbachev, decided to withdraw from Afghanistan. Agreement was reached in Geneva in 1988 and the last Soviet soldiers left Afghanistan in February 1989. Over 20,000 Soviet troops had died in ten years of fighting. Under Gorbachev, the media could report the war honestly (see Sources B and C).

The consequences were far greater for Afghanistan itself. About a million Afghans may have died – and the fighting went on even after the Soviet departure. By 1989, almost half the original Afghan population had become refugees. Those who were left could no longer grow enough food because the war had destroyed so much farmland.

A SOURCE

One Russian mother tried to discover how her soldier son died. She was told the following.

You cannot walk around saying that your son has been killed in Afghanistan. That's classified (secret) information.

B SOURCE

Aless Adamovich, writing in *Moscow News*, a Russian newspaper (1990).

The Afghan people lost a million lives in a war which we had no right to get involved in. We couldn't defeat the Afghan 'bandits' because they were fighting us as invaders.

C SOURCE

One Soviet soldier who fought in Afghanistan said the following afterwards:

We were given medals which we don't wear. When the time comes we'll return them. Those medals [were] received honestly in a dishonest war.

Question

Why did relations between the USA and the USSR worsen following the Soviet invasion of Afghanistan? [7 marks]

An Afghan boy and his mother collecting scrap from ruined houses (1995).

14 THE NEW COLD WAR

Key Issue

- Why did détente collapse in the early 1980s?

DÉTENTE UNDER THREAT

In 1980, America elected Ronald Regan as its new president. Reagan was fiercely anti-communist and this quickly led to a further deterioration in relations between the Soviet Union and the United States. However, the situation of détente between the two **superpowers** was already under threat before Reagan took over the presidency in 1981.

AFRICA

From the mid-1970s, the civil war in the former Portuguese colonies of Angola and Mozambique provided the Soviet Union with an opportunity to extend its influence into new regions of Africa. Angola became the focus of Cold War tension because of its oil resources. The Russians provided weapons and 50,000 Cuban troops to the **Marxist** MPLA (Popular Movement for the Liberation of Angola) faction while South Africa and America backed the anti-communist forces. The civil war continued into the 1990s despite the end of the Cold War.

CENTRAL AMERICA

In 1978, Soviet influence also extended into Central America. The Sandinistas, a Marxist guerrilla group, attacked and overthrew the pro-US government in Nicaragua. Soviet influence in Central America was of even more concern to the United States because it was that much closer to them.

THE 'EVIL EMPIRE'

The Soviet invasion of Afghanistan in 1979 brought an end to a decade which saw several setbacks for the United States. President Carter's responses to these were considered too soft by Reagan. Carter had refused to sell the American grain to the Russians and had **boycotted** the 1980 Olympic games held in Moscow. Reagan was determined to turn events America's way more decisively as the new Cold War gathered pace.

Reagan made clear his determination to confront the Soviet Union by approving the development of the neutron bomb. The neutron bomb killed people but did not destroy buildings. He also announced a $32 billion increase in the defence budget and decided to deploy Cruise and Pershing missiles in Europe. These were intermediate-range missiles which could not be spotted by enemy radar. For good measure, just in case the Soviets had not got the message, Reagan called the USSR the 'evil empire'. These developments all seemed to make a war that little bit more likely.

Despite this, the USA and the USSR began new arms talks in Geneva in July 1982. These were called START (Strategic Arms Reduction Talks). The two sides discussed limiting intermediate nuclear weapons in Europe.

STRATEGIC DEFENCE INITIATIVE

However, Reagan continued to keep the pressure on the Soviet Union. In 1983, he announced the beginning of the Strategic Defence Initiative (SDI). The

'Contra' guerrillas in Nicaragua, 1980. These were the anti-communist fighters equipped by Reagan.

How strategic warheads grew, 1964–74.

plan was to build a laser shield around the United States which would have made it impossible for Soviet missiles to hit American targets. People nicknamed it 'Star Wars'. Star Wars was controversial because it suggested that the US no longer accepted the principle of **MAD**. Reagan seemed to be suggesting that the United States could wage a nuclear war and survive.

In fact, the United States did not have the technology to make Star Wars a real possibility, but the Soviet Union did not know this and was greatly worried. The Soviet delegation walked out of the START negotiations in protest. The options facing the USSR were not encouraging. They knew they did not have the technology to match the SDI project and neither did they have the funds to pay for the research. Their only choice was to come to terms with Reagan.

1	Build up US defences, making it too expensive for the USSR to keep up
2	Stop western and Japanese technology getting into the USSR
3	More use of US radio stations, such as Radio Free Europe
4	Financial aid to communist countries which protect human rights
5	Secret help for reform movements in Poland, Hungary and Czechoslovakia

Reagan's plan to undermine the USSR.

ENTER GORBACHEV

Fortunately, from 1985 the Russians had a new leader who was willing to face this fact head on. Mikhail Gorbachev knew that the future of the communist system and the Soviet Union depended on its ability to deliver a higher standard of living to its people. It could not afford to spend huge sums of money on the military in order to compete with the United States. Gorbachev's Foreign Minister, Eduard Shevernadze, later calculated that as much as 50% of the Soviet Union's national income was spent on defence, arms and the armed forces. At the same time, the United States was spending just 6%.

Questions

a Study Source A. Explain the message of this cartoon, which shows Brezhnev riding on a dove, the symbol of peace. Support your answer by referring to details of the cartoon and your own knowledge. [6 marks]

b Explain why the process of détente had come to an end by 1981. [9 marks]

A SOURCE

A British cartoon of 1978. Soviet planes had attacked a Korean airliner which strayed into Russian airspace.

"If this is detente, heaven help us in a cold war!"

Key Issue

- How did the Soviet Union's economic problems affect the Cold War?

The Soviet economy was in a bad state when Gorbachev took over. Soviet leaders boasted that there was no **inflation**. In fact, there was – but no one knew how much. Official figures about the economy were false – but hardly anyone knew what the real ones were. The quality of consumer goods was very poor. Between 1982 and 1987, 18,000 Russian-made televisions exploded, killing 1000 people. In the West there were endless jokes about Soviet-made Lada motor cars:

Q. 'Why do Ladas have heated rear windows?'
A. 'To keep your hands warm when you're pushing them.'

Industrial production was falling and the military budget was out of control: no one really knew how much the armed forces cost. The communist system was corrupt – and no one knew how much that cost either.

There was really only one solution. As a leading communist pointed out, 'They had to drop out of the arms race'.

ARMS AGREEMENT (1987)

Gorbachev came to power in March 1985. In November, he met Reagan in Geneva. The two leaders agreed in principle to cut offensive weapons by 50 per cent. They would also try to limit medium-range missiles. 'The world has become a safer place,' Gorbachev told reporters afterwards.

It was a promising start. But the 1986 summit in Iceland broke down over Star Wars, which the USA refused to give up. However, Gorbachev confirmed that the USSR would withdraw from Afghanistan and promised that the USSR would not test any more nuclear weapons in the atmosphere unless the USA did so.

Success eventually came in December 1987 when the two leaders agreed to get rid of all medium- and short-range nuclear weapons. Reagan formally signed the INF (Intermediate Nuclear Forces) treaty on a visit to the Kremlin. It was an

amazing turnaround. He had been determined to stand up to the communists. Now, he signed the first agreement with them to reduce nuclear weapons. The dismantling of these weapons began at once.

Destroying a Titan II missile as part of the Salt II treaty.

GLASNOST AND PERESTROIKA

However, there had been arms agreements before and the Cold War had gone on. This time was different because Gorbachev had other plans. Arms cuts saved money but they did not solve the USSR's economic problems. And solving those, it turned out, was to end the Cold War in a dramatic fashion.

A Soviet report of 1983 had said that the Soviet economy was not working – and could not work without huge changes. There had to be more small businesses and co-operatives; people needed to be given greater freedom. The country needed to be more democratic.

It was a radical plan but Gorbachev used it as the basis for his new policies. He called these *glasnost* (openness) and *perestroika* (renewal). He wanted Soviet people to speak more openly and he encouraged Soviet leaders to listen to criticism.

In 1985, Gorbachev believed these two policies would reform the Soviet system. If corruption could be stamped out and everyone did their job properly, **communism** could be made to work. He soon discovered that he was wrong (see Source A).

Gorbachev wanted *perestroika*: he wished to rebuild the Soviet state. He eventually realised that this meant radical reforms in the Communist Party, too. However, he may not have realised how many people wanted to go further and get rid of the Communist Party altogether.

Gorbachev and Reagan in Moscow's Red Square (1988).

NO TANKS

This was especially true elsewhere in eastern Europe. The policy of *glasnost* encouraged people to criticise the system – the communist system. In the USSR's satellite countries, people deeply disliked both their own communist leaders and Soviet interference. In Hungary and Czechoslovakia, many people had bitter memories of how Soviet tanks had destroyed their attempts at freedom.

In March 1986, a crowd of 3000 marched through the streets of Budapest. They were celebrating Hungary's unofficial independence day. (The communists had stopped celebrating this after World War II.) They demanded more **democracy** (see Source B). At first, the police left them alone but, later, they used truncheons to beat up demonstrators.

There was, of course, another way to save communism: tanks. The USSR had used them in Hungary in 1956 and Czechoslovakia in 1968. The question in many people's minds was: would Gorbachev, too, use tanks to stop people gaining their freedom?

The answer, they discovered, was 'no' and Poland led the way in finding out.

This poster represents workers as bees, producing honey (money).

A SOURCE

Aleksandr Yakovlev was a key adviser to Gorbachev. In 1995, he said the following.

It seemed to us that all we had to do was remove some brakes, free it all up and it would all start working. There is a good engine there. It's got a bit old and rusty. It needs some oil. Just press the starter and it will set off down the track.

We went under this illusion for [up to] two years. But when we began to make radical changes in foreign policy we came up against the resistance of the system. That's when we began to understand that if we wanted radical reforms we would inevitably come up against the resistance of the system. From that moment it began to be said that the system is unreformable, the [Communist] Party is unreformable.

B SOURCE

One Young Communist League official was on the march. He said the following afterwards.

The only way to save socialism [communism] from the rubbish heap of history is to allow other groups in society, eventually other parties, to compete against the Party. Only if people choose it, is it worth having.

Questions

a **What progress towards arms reduction did Reagan and Gorbachev make? [4 marks]**
b **Explain why the Soviet economy was in such a poor state when Gorbachev took over as leader. [6 marks]**
c **Explain how the following together contributed to détente between the Soviet Union and the United States in the later 1980s:**
  • **Gorbachev's policy of *glasnost***
  • **The cost of spending on weapons**
  • **The INF Treaty, 1987.**
  [10 marks]

16 POLAND (1980–9)

Key Issue

- What was Poland's role in bringing about the end of communism in eastern Europe?

POLAND: COMMUNISM IN CRISIS

Nuclear missiles were not Reagan's only answer to the 'evil empire'. He was also making secret plans to destroy the Soviet Union's empire once and for all, starting with Poland. Poland was a good choice. The Poles had disliked the Russians for at least two centuries. Also, the Roman Catholic Church was a powerful force in the country. About 80% of Poles were Catholic. From 1945 onwards, the Church had served as a reminder that **communism** was not the only thing to believe in.

By 1980, the Polish economy was in serious trouble. Workers went on strike as a protest at high prices, and food and fuel shortages. At the shipyard in Gdansk, workers demanded pay rises and improved benefits. They also wanted the right to form a free trade union which could negotiate working conditions with the government.

Their wish was granted: in August, Poland became the first eastern communist country to have a free trade union. It was called Solidarity. The leader of its ten million members was Lech Walesa. The USSR did not send troops in, partly because of world criticism of its invasion of Afghanistan. Also, late in 1980, the USA warned Brezhnev that, if the USSR invaded Poland, the USA would sell weapons to China.

SECRET AGREEMENT

But Soviet leaders were worried and ordered a crackdown on the protesters. In December 1981, the Polish armed forces took over the government and General Jaruzelski became Polish leader. Riot police moved in with water cannons and troops used tear gas to break up meetings. Solidarity's leaders were put in prison. In 1982, the union was banned.

That might have been the end of the matter, but in June 1982 a unique meeting took place between US President Reagan and Pope John Paul II. He had become Pope in 1978 and he was Polish.

The two men believed they could work together to keep Solidarity alive. They planned to do it by secretly undermining the Polish government (see Source B). An American adviser described it as 'one of the great secret alliances of all time'.

They believed that, as a result, the USSR would lose its grip on Poland and the country could regain its freedom. If Poland became free, other communist states might follow.

From 1982–9, various western organisations provided money to help the banned union. Some of it came from the CIA. Solidarity also received equipment, smuggled into Poland by priests and foreign trade unions. It included telephones, transmitters, computers and video cameras.

Above all, Solidarity received advice on how to deal with the Polish government and the USSR. This advice was based on secret information which the USA received from Polish priests and even spies in the Polish government.

Solidarity's advice to workers to help create chaos (1982).

THE POPE'S ROLE

When the USSR did not invade Poland in 1980, it was another turning-point in the Cold War. But Poland's path to democracy over the next ten years was not a smooth one. Solidarity was banned in October 1982, although prisoners were released soon afterwards. The Pope played a key part in achieving this.

In return for promising to visit his native Poland, Pope John Paul II insisted that:

- **martial law** should end;
- prisoners should be released;
- there should be independent trade unions.

Poland's leader, General Jaruzelski, introduced reforms to improve the economy and began to work more closely with the Catholic Church. Meanwhile, support for the Communist Party was falling: half of its members left. Those who stayed in the party were mostly Catholics and many read the underground newspapers. They would not have been Lenin's idea of typical communists.

B SOURCE

Ronald Reagan, speaking in the 1990s.

We both felt that a great mistake had been made at Yalta and something should be done. Solidarity was the very weapon for bringing this about, because it was an organisation of the labourers of Poland.

Questions

a Study Source A. Explain the importance of this photograph. Support your answer by referring to details of the photograph and your own knowledge. [6 marks]
b Explain why Solidarity played such a key role in the defeat of communism in Poland. [9 marks]

Explain how communism began to collapse in eastern Europe. Write a few sentences under the following headings:
- Soviet invasion of Afghanistan
- 'Star Wars'
- Crisis in the Soviet economy
- Role of Gorbachev
- INF Treaty.

A SOURCE

Gdansk strikers at prayer, August 1980.

THE EFFECT OF GORBACHEV

Both the Polish government and Solidarity supported Gorbachev's *glasnost* and *perestroika*. Indeed, the union had wanted these reforms for some years. The communists were anxious to show they supported Gorbachev because they wanted to hold on to power.

But the government had become weak. At the first sign of opposition, it was willing to change its policies.

SOLIDARITY LEGALISED

However, something was happening to the Polish economy: it was getting worse. Prices were rising and living standards were falling. The country owed huge sums of money abroad and could not afford to replace old industrial machinery. Production was falling. In 1988, an opinion poll showed that about a quarter of Poles wanted to emigrate to the West.

In January 1988, there were more strikes in protest at Poland's poor economic record. Workers demanded that Solidarity should be made legal again. Lech Walesa asked for talks with the government and the government agreed (see Source B).

The talks lasted for two months. In April 1989, a deal was struck: Solidarity would be made legal and workers would have the right to strike. More importantly, there would be new elections. Two-thirds of the seats in the Sejm (parliament) would be guaranteed for communists and their allies; one-third could be contested by other parties.

THE END OF COMMUNISM IN POLAND

Of course, the system was designed so that the communists would win. Despite this, it was an historic decision: the government had agreed to hold free elections for the first time since the war. They were also the first free elections in any communist country.

When the election was held, Solidarity won all 161 seats open to opposition parties. This left Poland in a strange position: the communists did not have the people's support; Solidarity did not have enough MPs to run the country. In effect, the communist leadership stayed in control.

But not for long. Jaruzelski (now President) tried to get Solidarity to join a coalition government but Walesa refused. Instead, two weeks later, Solidarity formed a coalition with two other parties and won a majority of votes in the Sejm.

The following day, Jaruzelski appointed a new government, which included Solidarity MPs. The new prime minister was Tadeusz Mazowiecki, a non-communist and Roman Catholic. It was the first non-communist Polish government since the Second World War – and the first in any Soviet satellite.

August 1989: Solidarity leader, Lech Walesa.

EFFECT ON THE COLD WAR

The Cold War had happened partly because the USSR and USA had very different systems – communism and capitalism. To defend their views, each side had built up huge amounts of weapons. And each side had its supporters – the USA was supported by western Europe while the USSR was supported by eastern Europe.

But this situation was changing. Both sides had already agreed to arms cuts. If eastern Europe rejected communism, another reason for the 'war' would have disappeared. In the summer of 1989, Poland did reject communism – and Hungary was not far behind.

HUNGARY

In May 1988, Karoly Grosz took over from János Kádár as Communist Party leader and there were big changes in the Party leadership. In January 1989, the government decided to rebury Imre Nagy (see page 15). Days later, it announced that an enquiry into the events of 1956 had shown that it had not been a 'counter-revolution' after all. They decided that it had actually been a popular uprising.

Early in 1989, it was agreed that other political parties should be allowed. Instead of sending in tanks to stop this, Gorbachev did the opposite: he agreed to start withdrawing troops from Hungary.

WHY?

When Gorbachev came to power, he knew that the USSR had to find new ways of dealing with eastern Europe. So he abandoned the Brezhnev Doctrine (see page 34). In future, east Europeans would be treated as partners. The USSR would not send in tanks; instead, Gorbachev believed that each country should sort out its own problems (see Source C).

A SOURCE

Communism's solution to huge queues for scarce goods for sale was not to have anything to sell, as you can see from this photograph, taken in 1981. A lack of quality consumer goods was a serious problem for the communist economies.

B SOURCE

Walesa told those at the talks the following.

There is only one direction. It must go towards a democratic system, towards the rule of law and the freedom of its citizens. Even if we cannot get all that, we have to start somewhere.

C SOURCE

Gennady Gerasimov, one of Gorbachev's advisers, explained the new policy in autumn 1989.

The new doctrine is Frank Sinatra's doctrine. Frank Sinatra has a very popular song, 'I had it my way'. So Hungary, Poland, any other countries has it its own way. They decide which road to take. It's their business.

Questions

a Study Source A. Explain the importance of this photograph. Support your answer by referring to details of the photograph and your own knowledge. [6 marks]

b Explain why Poland became the first East European state to have a non-communist government. [9 marks]

17 THE END OF COMMUNISM

Key Issue

• How did communism in Europe end?

THE BERLIN WALL DESTROYED

In May 1989, Hungary took down the barbed-wire fence along its Austrian border: people could now travel from East to West. About 20,000 East Germans fled to the West before the border was officially opened in September. The East German leader, Erich Honecker, tried to hold back the tide and stay in power. But, without Soviet support, there was little he could do and he resigned in October.

The East Berlin communist leader announced that the Berlin Wall would be opened on 9 November. At midnight on 8–9 November, thousands celebrated as the gates were opened. People hacked at the wall with pickaxes to take home a souvenir. The Iron Curtain's most famous landmark would soon be just a heap of rubble.

The rest of communist Europe could not avoid the effects. On 10 November, the Bulgarian president resigned after holding power for 33 years. Later that month, demonstrations in Czechoslovakia toppled the communist government without bloodshed.

By contrast, the revolution in Romania was a violent affair. A civil war raged for four days between the Romanian army and supporters of Nicolae Ceausescu, the country's unpopular president. Eventually, he was captured and executed by firing squad on Christmas Day 1989.

THE END OF THE COLD WAR

Reagan retired in 1989 as the most popular president in American history. The new president, George Bush, met Gorbachev on 3 December 1989. They made an historic announcement: the Cold War was over.

However, changes continued to sweep through eastern Europe during 1990. In March, talks began in Berlin on the reunification of East and West Germany. Britain, France, the USA and USSR later signed a treaty which gave back full powers to East and West Germany as independent nations. In October, they were reunited after 45 years. Meanwhile, East Berlin's History Museum locked up the display which covered the years 1949–61.

In April 1990, communist rule in Hungary ended when voters chose the Hungarian Democratic Forum to lead the new government. Yugoslavia, too, held its first multi-party elections that month. Even Albania, the most Stalinist of the East European states, took its first steps towards the end of communist rule when the ban on opposition parties was ended in December. In the summer of 1991, they actually joined the government.

START TREATY SIGNED (1991)

In August, Gorbachev and Bush finally signed START after nine years of talks. They agreed to destroy about one-third of their nuclear weapons. They signed the agreement with pens made from scrapped missiles.

An image people never expected to see: Ronald Reagan speaking below the bust of Lenin (1988).

An image people never expected to see: Hungary sold its part of the Iron Curtain as souvenirs.

THE END OF THE USSR (1991)

In August 1991, there was an attempted coup against Mikhail Gorbachev by hard-line communists. It failed mainly because the new Russian President, Boris Yeltsin, opposed it. He urged soldiers to mutiny and workers to strike in protest. Thousands took to the Moscow streets.

Just four days later, Yeltsin suspended the Communist Party in Russia. As one ordinary Russian wrote to a Soviet newspaper, 'The world has moved on. The Party didn't make good use of 72 years.'

After the coup failed, many Soviet republics decided they wanted to be independent and not controlled by Moscow. One of them was Russia itself, led by Boris Yeltsin. In December, the Soviet state finally broke up. Gorbachev resigned as Soviet President, as there was no longer a Soviet state to be president of.

As he announced his resignation on television, the communist red flag was lowered for the last time over the Kremlin. Gorbachev said, 'The old system fell apart before the new one began to work.' The 'evil empire' which Reagan had wanted to destroy, had destroyed itself.

A SOURCE

An image people never expected to see: the Berlin Wall is torn down (1989).

An image people never expected to see: Gorbachev speaking in 1992 in Fulton, Missouri, where Churchill first spoke of an 'iron curtain' in 1946.

Questions

a Study Source A. Explain the importance of this photograph. Support your answer by referring to details of the photograph and your own knowledge. [6 marks]

b Why did the Soviet Union cease to exist in 1991? [9 marks]

18 THE COLD WAR'S LEGACY

Key Issue

- What effects did the Cold War have?

As the Iron Curtain tumbled, so the secrets came spilling out. For instance, in 1991, Gorbachev and Bush agreed to take nuclear bombers off alert and put nuclear warheads in storage.

It sounded very impressive. It seemed to reduce the risk of nuclear war. In fact, there was nothing new in this agreement. The arrangement had secretly existed for decades.

Accidents in the USA in 1966 and 1968 had led to all American bombers being grounded until the end of the Cold War. Soviet planes had never carried nuclear weapons for safety reasons. For years, they had been loading up dummy ones!

START II SIGNED (1993)

In 1993, Yeltsin and Bush signed the START II Treaty which brought further cuts in the stocks of US and Russian missiles. However, it still left both countries with about one-third of their long-range warheads – over 6000 of them.

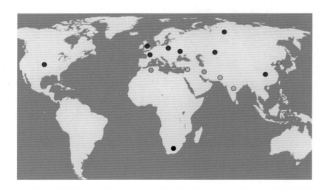

Key
- Countries which have nuclear weapons / USA, Russia, Ukraine, Britain, France, China, Belarus, Kazakhstan
- Countries which probably have them / India, Pakistan, Israel
- Countries possibly developing them / Algeria, Iran, North Korea
- Countries which had them / South Africa

The nuclear threat: who had nuclear weapons or could make them?

Yet the risk of nuclear war remained because nuclear missiles still existed – not just in the USSR and the USA but in many smaller countries, too.

NATIONALISM

The decline of **communism** led to the return of an old danger, nationalism. Throughout the communist bloc, many people were not satisfied with **democracy**: they wanted their own independent nation too.

Latvia, Estonia and Lithuania all became independent in 1991 and joined the United Nations. In January 1993, Czechoslovakia peacefully split to become two separate states of the Czech Republic and Slovakia.

In the former USSR, fighting broke out as a number of areas tried to win independence.

CIVIL WAR IN YUGOSLAVIA

However, the worst violence occurred in what had been Yugoslavia. Tito had held together an explosive mixture of Serbs, Croats and Muslims, but communist control collapsed in 1990. The following year, the Serbs refused to accept a Croat as leader and both Slovenia and Croatia declared independence.

Key

Serbs	Macedonians
Croats	Albanians
Muslims	Hungarians
Slovenes	Bulgarians
Montenegrins	Romanians / Slovaks

Who controlled what in the former Yugoslavia?

During the civil war which followed, the Serbian government used a policy which they called 'ethnic cleansing'. This meant removing non-Serbs from mainly Serb areas – or killing them. Apart from the deaths, up to 20,000 Muslim and Croat women and girls were raped.

The United Nations brokered a ceasefire in Croatia in 1992. It was the first of many in the region but 40,000 UN troops failed to keep the peace. One Serb soldier gave this chilling warning: 'The time of living together is over'. NATO forces then launched air-strikes against Serbia in 1995 after the Serbs refused to surrender any Bosnian territory, eventually leading to a peace agreement which created separate states for Serbia, Croatia and Bosnia. The Serbs got 49% of Bosnia, the Croats and Muslims 51%.

KOREA

Korea was one of the Cold War's first trouble spots. It is also one of the last. North Korea remains communist whilst South Korea is capitalist. Anti-aircraft guns in Seoul, the South Korean capital, are still permanently guarded, ready for a North Korean attack. A narrow **demilitarised** zone separates the two sides. Every day at noon, both sides meet to settle disputes, such as shooting incidents.

VIETNAM

In 1993, the French President said that the French had made a 'mistake' in fighting in Vietnam. In the USA, the arguments about American involvement in Vietnam go on. Robert McNamara was US Defence Secretary under Presidents Kennedy and Johnson. In 1995, he admitted that his handling of the war had been 'terribly wrong'.

It led to a new round of arguments about the war. The USA has not forgotten Vietnam because it has not yet recovered from the experience. Vietnam was the war the Americans lost. What many still wonder is whether they should have been fighting in the first place. On the other hand, many Americans argue that the USA lost the war in Vietnam – but won the battle against communism.

EASTERN EUROPE

What about the people of eastern Europe? Are they satisfied with their new lives? A poll early in 1993 showed that over half the people in the former USSR thought they had been better off under communism. About 70 per cent in eastern Europe were not satisfied with democracy. And 10 per cent wanted to emigrate to the West. Today many could have this wish, as most of the old Soviet bloc countries, such as Poland, Hungary and the Czech Republic, joined the European Union in May 2004 and now their citizens have the right to work in western Europe.

A beggar in Moscow.

THE COLD WAR'S COST

It is impossible to say what the Cold War cost. Billions of dollars and roubles were spent on building nuclear weapons. Defence budgets in the USA and USSR soaked up money which might have been used to improve living standards. Now that the Cold War is over, many more billions are being spent on getting rid of these weapons.

Nor have all the debts been paid yet. The cost of sorting out the ex-USSR's economy has been estimated at nearly $2 trillion a year. However much help the West gives, the Russians and others will have to pay for most of it on their own.

However, the first half of the twentieth century saw two world wars. In the second half, there were none. Some people believe that this was partly because both superpowers had nuclear weapons – but were afraid to use them. At the beginning of the twenty-first century, Europe and the United States have new issues to concern them – most notably, the threat of global terrorism. The Cold War has become a dim memory.

Explain how the Cold War came to an end. Write a few sentences under each of the following headings:
- Gorbachev's rejection of the Brezhnev Doctrine
- The pulling down of the Berlin Wall
- Collapse of communism in the USSR
- Tensions in the 1990s.

QUESTION 1

A SOURCE

A history textbook on the spread of communism in eastern Europe (from *World History, 1914–80*, Peter Neville, 1982).

The Red Army remained in occupation of the liberated territories, and it became increasingly clear that the local communist parties had Moscow's full backing in their drive to achieve power. In Poland, for example, Stalin went back on the promise given at Yalta that there would be free elections.

B SOURCE

A British cartoon on the Berlin Blockade, July 1948, showing Stalin in a chimney.

THE BIRD WATCHER

Questions

a Describe the decisions concerning Germany made at the Yalta Conference of 1945. [6 marks]

b What does Source A tell us about how Stalin gained control of the liberated territories of Eastern Europe? [3 marks]

c How reliable is Source B to an historian studying the Berlin Blockade? Use Source B and your own knowledge to explain your answer. [6 marks]

d In what ways did relations between the Soviet Union and the Western powers change between 1945–9? [10 marks]

QUESTION 2

A SOURCE

British cartoon from *Punch* magazine, 31 October 1956. It shows Khrushchev trying to train the 'bears' of Eastern Europe.

B SOURCE

A report from a journalist for the British newspaper, *The Daily Mail*, at the time of the Hungarian Rising, November 1956.

As I moved deeper into the city, every street was smashed. Hardly a stretch of tramcar rails was left intact. Hundreds of yards of paving stones had been torn up, the streets were littered with burnt-out cars. Even before I reached the hotel, I counted the carcasses of at least 40 tanks. At the corner of Stalin Avenue, two monster Russian T54 tanks lumbered past, dragging bodies behind them; a warning to all Hungarians of what happened to fighters.

Questions

a **Describe the relations between the Soviet Union and the European communist states up to and including 1956. [6 marks]**
b **What does Source A tell us about relations between the Soviet Union and the European communist states? [3 marks]**
c **How reliable is Source B to an historian studying the Hungarian Rising of 1956? Use Source B and your own knowledge to explain your answer. [6 marks]**
d **Which was the more serious threat to Soviet control of Eastern Europe:**
  • **The Hungarian Rising, 1956; or**
  • **Events in Czechoslovakia, 1968?**
  You must refer to both reasons when explaining your answer. [10 marks]

A SOURCE

Alex Bovin, writing in *Izvestia*, a Soviet newspaper (1980).

The Soviet Union was forced to make a choice: we had to bring in troops or let the Afghan [pro-communist] revolution be defeated. We knew that the decision to bring in troops would not be popular, even if it was legal. But we also knew that we would have ceased to be a great power if we [did not take] unpopular but necessary decisions.

B SOURCE

An American cartoon from 1985, showing Uncle Sam (the symbol of the USA) and Nicaragua (see page 38).

Questions

a Describe why relations between the Soviet Union and the United States became worse in the early 1980s. [6 marks]

b What does Source A tell us about why the USSR invaded Afghanistan in 1979? [3 marks]

c How reliable is Source B to an historian studying US involvement in Nicaragua in the early 1980s? Use Source B and your own knowledge to explain your answer. [6 marks]

d Which was more important as a reason for increasing Cold War tension in the years 1979–83:
• the Soviet invasion of Afghanistan, 1979; or
• US plans to develop 'Star Wars' technology, 1983?
You must refer to both reasons in your answer. [10 marks]

QUESTION 4

A SOURCE

A letter to the New York *Daily Mirror* newspaper in 1957, during Khrushchev's visit to the United States; quoted in *Inside Russia Today*, John Gunther, 1957.

There have been lots of complaints about Khrushchev's appearance on CBS TV. It seems many think he pulled a terrific propaganda job on the American people.

Well, I was right there in my living room watching this Red Butcher, with a few million other Americans, and he left me cold!

Everyone knows a sneak and a liar can't look you straight in the eye, and while Khrushchev talked the usual Commie yap-trap about peace and love, not once did he look directly into the TV cameras . . . The only thing he sold me on was that he was a sly, slippery liar that didn't have the guts to look his TV audience in the eye.

Questions

a According to Source A, why were some Americans unhappy about Khrushchev appearing on US television? [3 marks]
b How reliable is the view of Khrushchev given in Source A? Use Source A and your own knowledge to answer this question. [6 marks]
c Describe how Khrushchev's coming to power in the Soviet Union affected relations with the United States. [6 marks]
d Why did rivalry between the USA and the Soviet Union increase in the period 1945–55? [10 marks]

QUESTION 5

A SOURCE

Description of life in the Soviet Union just before the end of communism; from *The End of the American Century*, Jeffrey Robinson, 1997.

The winter before August 1991, food shortages brought the Russians to the point of total desperation. The following winter, things were even worse. At one point there was no milk. When there was milk, there was no meat. When there was fruit juice, there was no toilet paper. Factories closed because there was no heat. Communism turned out to be the worst economic disaster in the history of the world. Until recently, everything was always sold at a loss. A loaf of bread used to cost 20 kopeks to buy but 60 kopeks to bake.

B SOURCE

President Reagan, speaking during a 1988 television programme.

I told Mr Gorbachev, 'We don't mistrust each other because . . . we're armed this way. We're armed this way because we mistrust each other. And if you and I can eliminate the reasons for this mistrust, the arms will take care of themselves'.

Questions

a What can you learn from Source A about the Soviet economy? [3 marks]
b How did the problems of the Soviet economy in the 1980s contribute to the end of communism in the Soviet Union? [6 marks]
c How reliable to an historian is the view of Reagan's attitude towards the Cold War given in Source B? Use Source B and your own knowledge to answer this question. [6 marks]
d Which was the more important reason for the collapse of communism in eastern Europe:
  • the role of Solidarity in Poland; or
  • Gorbachev's policy of *glasnost* in the Soviet Union?
You must refer to both reasons when explaining your answer. [10 marks]

B SOURCE

An American cartoon about President Nixon's policy of Vietnamisation.

A SOURCE

An Australian journalist, Wilfred G Burchett, describes the Berlin Blockade in his book, *The Cold War in Germany*, 1950.

When the transport restrictions to Berlin were imposed, when factories were closing down in the western sector, when parks and gardens were being robbed of their trees for fuel, when the West Berliners had two hours of gas and electricity per day, Ebert, the mayor of the Soviet sector of Berlin, offered to supply all the food, coal and power that West Berlin needed.

Reuter, the mayor of West Berlin, turned down the offer. The crisis had to continue. The greater the misery, the colder and hungrier the West Berliners became, the more Reuter and his western advisers hoped to turn them against the Russians.

Questions

a Study Source A. Explain the point the author is making. Support your answer by referring to details in the source and your own knowledge. [6 marks]

b Explain why the crisis over Berlin during 1948–9 came about. [9 marks]

c What was agreed at the Potsdam Conference, 1945? [4 marks]

d Why did Churchill make his 'Iron Curtain' speech in 1946? [6 marks]

e Explain how the following together contributed to tension between the Soviet Union and the West in the years 1945–7:
- Soviet expansion in eastern Europe
- The Marshall Plan
- The Truman Doctrine. [10 marks]

Questions

a Study Source B. Explain the message of this cartoon. Support your answer by referring to details of the cartoon and your own knowledge. [6 marks]

b Explain how the Tet Offensive affected the outcome of the Vietnam War. [9 marks]

SOURCE

A cartoon showing Khrushchev on the Berlin Wall.

BERLIN WALL
ERECTED
AUG 13. 1961

Questions

a Study Source C. Explain the message of this cartoon. Support your answer by referring to details of the cartoon and your own knowledge. [6 marks]

b Explain why there was a crisis in 1961 over Berlin. [9 marks]

c What happened during the 'Prague Spring' of 1968? [4 marks]

d Explain why the USSR got involved in Czechoslovakia in 1968. [6 marks]

e Explain how the following together affected relations between the USA and the Soviet Union:
• The nuclear arms race
• Khrushchev becoming leader of the Soviet Union
• Tension over Berlin, 1961.
[10 marks]

D SOURCE

The Cuban Missiles Crisis as seen by the British magazine, *Punch*, 17 October, 1962. It shows Kennedy on the left and Khrushchev on the right.

OVER THE GARDEN WALL

E SOURCE

Cartoon from the British magazine, *Punch*, October 1961.

VITAL DISCUSSION

Questions

a Study Source D. Explain the message of this cartoon. Support your answer by referring to details of the cartoon and your own knowledge. [6 marks]

b How did relations between the USA and the Soviet Union change as a result of the Cuban Missiles Crisis? [9 marks]

c What was the Strategic Defence Initiative (Star Wars)? [4 marks]

d Explain how Gorbachev planned to change the Soviet Union. [6 marks]

e Explain how the following together contributed to the collapse of Soviet control over Eastern Europe:
  • Solidarity in Poland
  • Problems of the Soviet economy
  • Gorbachev's policy of *glasnost*.
    [10 marks]

Questions

a Study Source E. Explain the message of this cartoon. Support your answer by referring to details of the cartoon and your own knowledge. [6 marks]

b Why were relations between the USA and the Soviet Union particularly tense at the time of this cartoon? [9 marks]

F SOURCE

A British cartoon from 1968. It shows Brezhnev with the hammer and sickle symbol on his apron.

"Oliver Twist has asked for more!"— *Mr Bumble (Oliver Twist)*

Questions

a Study Source F. Explain the message of this cartoon. Support your answer by referring to details of the cartoon and your own knowledge. [6 marks]

b Explain why the Soviet Union invaded Czechoslovakia in 1968. [9 marks]

PART A-STYLE QUESTIONS

Questions

1 (i)   What was meant by the term 'satellite state'? [3 marks]
   (ii) Why was the Berlin Wall built in 1961? [5 marks]
   (iii) Describe the key features of the Prague Spring in 1968. [5 marks]
   (iv) Why was the Hungarian Rising in 1956 crushed by the Soviet Union? [7 marks]

2 (i)   Explain what is meant by the 'arms race'. [3 marks]
   (ii) Why was the North Atlantic Treaty Organisation (NATO) formed in 1949? [5 marks]
   (iii) Describe the key features of the Hungarian Uprising (1956). [5 marks]
   (iv) What were the effects of the Cuban Missiles Crisis on relations between the USA and USSR in the 1960s? [7 marks]

3 (i)   Give one reason to explain why the issue of the Second Front caused tension between the Soviet Union and the West. [3 marks]
   (ii) Describe the key features of the Yalta Conference. [5 marks]

   (iii) Why was the Truman Doctrine issued? [5 marks]
   (iv) Why was there tension over Berlin in 1948–9? [7 marks]

4 (i)   What was meant by 'the evil empire'? [3 marks]
   (ii) Why did the United States boycott the 1980 Olympic Games? [4 marks]
   (iii) Why did the USA threaten to develop SDI (Star Wars) in the 1980s? [6 marks]
   (iv) In what ways did President Gorbachev attempt to end the Cold War? [7 marks]

5 (i)   Give one reason why relations between the Soviet Union and the western Allies became more tense in 1945. [3 marks]
   (ii) How did the Allies deal with Germany's borders in 1945? [5 marks]
   (iii) Describe the key features of the Truman Doctrine. [5 marks]
   (iv) What were the effects of the Berlin Blockade on relations between the superpowers in the late 1940s? [7 marks]

PART B-STYLE QUESTIONS

Questions

1 (i) In what ways did relations between the USA and the USSR change in the years 1949–55? [10 marks]

(ii) Why did relations between the USA and the USSR change in the period from the end of the Second World War to the beginning of the Berlin Blockade (1948)?
You may use the following information to help you with your answer:
- the Yalta conference, 1945
- Churchill's Iron Curtain speech, 1946
- the Soviet takeover of eastern Europe
- the Berlin Blockade (1948).
[15 marks]

2 (i) Explain why there was a crisis over Cuba in 1962. [10 marks]

(ii) Why did relations between the USA and the USSR change in the years 1975–86?
You may use the following information to help you with your answer:
- Helsinki Agreement, 1975
- Invasion of Afghanistan, 1979
- USA begins 'Star Wars' development, 1983
- INF Treaty signed, 1986.
[15 marks]

3 (i) Why had a Cold War developed by 1949? [10 marks]

(ii) In what ways did relations change between the USA and the USSR in the years 1949–56?
You may use the following information to help in your answer:
- The end of the Berlin Blockade, 1949
- The Korean War, 1950–3
- The death of Stalin, 1953
- The Hungarian Rising, 1956.
[15 marks]

4 (i) Why did relations between the USA and the USSR change in the years 1979–80? [10 marks]

(ii) In what ways did the USA and the USSR try to reduce Cold War tensions in the years 1963–79?
You may use the following information to help you with your answer:
- Nuclear Test Ban Treaty
- End of the Vietnam War
- The Helsinki Agreement
- SALT I and SALT II.
[15 marks]

AFTERWORD

Afghanistan   Fighting continued until the victory of an Islamic fundamentalist group, the Taliban. These, in turn, were defeated by the United States in 2002.

Atom Bomb   It was revealed in 1994 that four of the main nine inventors of the atom bomb gave information to the USSR about it in the years after 1945.

Baltic States   Latvia, Estonia and Lithuania became independent in 1991 and joined the UN.

Berlin   The Allied occupying troops left Berlin in 1994. The British HQ, originally built for the 1936 Olympics, is a rare surviving complete example of Nazi architecture. It is protected by a preservation order.

Berlin Wall   Most of the 224,000 tons of concrete panels were ground down and sold as building materials. However, 100 metres of it was bought by the New York Museum of Modern Art. Another section now stands outside CIA head quarters.

Czechoslovakia   Czechoslovakia split to become the two separate states of Slovakia and the Czech Republic on 1 January 1993.

Alexander Dubcek   In 1989, Dubcek was elected President of the Czech Parliament after the Czech revolution. In 1990, he was received at the Kremlin by Gorbachev. He died after a car crash in 1992. Many people were suspicious about the circumstances of his death. General Salgovic, the man who arrested him in 1968, committed suicide soon after the 1989 Czech revolution.

Erich Honecker   The former East German leader was put on trial in 1992 for the manslaughter of people who had died trying to cross the Berlin Wall. The charges were dropped on humanitarian grounds.

Korea   Anti-aircraft guns in Seoul, South Korea, are still permanently manned, ready for a North Korean attack. There is a daily meeting in the demilitarised zone to settle disputes. Under a 1994 agreement, North Korea gave up its nuclear programme in return for two nuclear reactors and free fuel oil. Kim Il Sung, North Korean dictator and the world's longest-serving political leader, died the same year.

Imre Nagy   In June 1989, Imre Nagy's body was reburied, along with four others. A sixth coffin was empty – it represented all the others who died in the 1956 revolution. Three weeks later, the Hungarian Supreme Court ruled that Nagy had been innocent.

North Vietnam   The USA established formal links with North Vietnam in 1995, 20 years after they left South Vietnam.

Poland   The body of Paderewski, Poland's first Prime Minister, who died in New York in 1941, was reburied in Warsaw in 1992.

Russia   It is now possible to buy pictures of nuclear sites from the Defence Ministry for $1500. Low-grade secrets are also for sale. In 1994, Queen Elizabeth II visited Russia. She was the first reigning British monarch to do so.

Saigon   The US embassy in Saigon is now partly occupied by the Vietnam State Petroleum Company. The helicopter landing pad on the roof is still marked out, with the letter H in the centre. It was from there that the last Americans in South Vietnam were airlifted in 1975.

Vietnam War   By 1995, US investigators had received proof that most missing US servicemen were dead.

Warsaw Pact   This was dissolved in 1991. Since then, Poland, Hungary, Lithuania, the Czech Republic and Slovakia have all become members of the EU.

Allies – Britain, the USA and the USSR during the Second World War

Armistice – a break in fighting

Autobahn – motorway

Blockade – shutting off a country or city from trade and travel links

Boycott – refusal to trade with, or have links to, a group or country

British Commonwealth – organisation representing countries formerly in the British Empire

Buffer zone – an area providing protection from invasion

Capitalist – supporter of private ownership of businesses

CIA – Central Intelligence Agency; US secret service

Coalition government – government consisting of two or more parties working together

Communism – state control of the economy

Constitution – set of rules by which a country is governed

Counter-revolution – a revolution against a revolution

Demilitarised – without troops or weapons

Democracy – system where governments are elected by the people

De-Stalinisation – ending of the harsh and repressive policies associated with Stalin

Draft law – law forcing men to do military service

Fascist – opponent of democracy and supporter of rule by one powerful leader with a strong military following

GI – American soldier

Glasnost – one of Gorbachev's reforms, encouraging debate and 'openness'

Guerrilla war – type of warfare based on hit-and-run tactics by unconventional fighters

ICBMs – Inter-Continental Ballistic Missile

Inflation – increase in prices

KGB – Soviet secret service

Labour camps – prisons for opponents of the government in the Soviet Union

MAD – Mutually Assured Destruction – the theory that a nuclear war would wipe out both sides

Martial law – rule by army

Marxist – supporter of Karl Marx's communist ideas

Nationalised – taken over by the state

Partisan – person who fought behind enemy lines

Party Congress – meeting of the representatives of the Soviet Communist Party

People's democracy – the communist countries of eastern Europe

Perestroika – one of Gorbachev's reforms, freeing up the Soviet economy and allowing competition

Profiteers – people who make excessive profits, usually on the black market

Red Army – army of the Soviet Union

Reparations – payments in compensation for damage

Resistance – secret opposition to those in power

Royalist – supporter of monarchy

Satellites – countries under another country's influence

Speculators – people taking a risk in buying or selling

Summit meeting – meeting of world leaders

Superpowers – the United States and the Soviet Union

United Nations – international organisation representing the world's countries

The publishers would like to thank the following individuals, institutions and companies for permission to reproduce copyright illustrations in this book: p5l Popperfoto, r Leslie Illingworth, *Daily Mail*, 6th March 1946, Centre for the Study of Cartoons and Caricature, University of Kent © Associated Newspapers/Solo Syndication; p6 Jim Pringle/Associated Press; p8 Associated Press; p9l Topham Picturepoint, r *Punch*; p10 Ullstein Bild, Berlin; p11 Fritz Reiss/AP Photo; p15 Popperfoto; p16 AKG Images; p18 Hulton-Deutsch Collection/Corbis; p20 Bettman/Corbis; p21 David Low, *Daily Herald*, 30th June 1950 Centre for the Study of Cartoons and Caricature, University of Kent © Associated Newspapers/ Solo Syndication; p24 Gamma/Katz; p25 & 26 Popperfoto; p27 Leslie Illingworth, *Daily Mail*, 29th October 1962, Centre for the Study of Cartoons and Caricature, University of Kent © Associated Newspapers/Solo Syndication; p29 AP Photo Library: p30 Bettman/Corbis; p31l Larry Burrows/Time Life Pictures/Getty Images, r AP Photo Library/Nick Ut; p32l AP Photo Library/Eddie Adams, r Topfoto; p33 Bleitreu Jason/Corbis Sygma; p34 Bettman Corbis; p35 Wally McNamee/Corbis; p36 Topham/AP; p38 Hulton Archive; p39 Michael Cummings/Express Newspapers; p40 Roger Ressmeyer/Corbis; p41t AP Photo Library/Ira Schwartz; p43 Sipa/Rex; p44 Peter Turnley/Corbis; p45 Bruno Barbey/Magnum; p46 Miroslav Zajic/Corbis; p47l James A Finley/Associated Press, r Reuters/Corbis; p49 Bojan Brecelj/Corbis; p50 & 51 *Punch*; p52 AUTH ©1985 The *Philadelphia Inquirer*. Reprinted with permission of UNIVERSAL PRESS SYNDI-CATE. All rights reserved; p54 Hartford Times; p56l & r Punch; p57 Stanley Franklin, *Daily Mirror* 26th July 1968, Centre for the Study of Cartoons and Caricature © Mirrorpix.

The publishers would also like to thank the following for material in this book: Penguin for extracts from *Overkill: The Story of Modern Weapons*, J Cox; Macdonald for extracts from *Kennedy*, R Gadney; Addison Wesley Longman for extracts from *Superpower Rivalry* by S Judges; Heinemann for extracts from *World History 1914–80*, P Neville; HarperCollins for extracts from *Inside Russia Today*, J Gunther; World Unity Publications for extracts from *The Cold War in Germany*, W G Burchett.
Exam questions reproduced with the kind permission of OCR and London Qualifications Ltd, trading as Edexcel.

Every effort has been made to trace and acknowledge ownership of copyright. The publishers will be glad to make suitable arrangements with any copyright holders whom it has not been possible to contact.

Orders: please contact Bookpoint Ltd, 130 Milton Park, Abingdon, Oxon OX14 4SB. Telephone: (44) 01235 827720. Fax: (44) 01235 400454. Lines are open from 9.00 – 5.00, Monday to Saturday, with a 24-hour message answering service. You can also order through our website www.hoddereducation.co.uk.

British Library Cataloguing in Publication Data
A catalogue record for this title is available from the British Library

ISBN–13: 978 0 340 81479 6

First Published 2005
Impression number   10 9 8 7 6 5
Year   2010 2009

Copyright © Neil DeMarco and John Aylett 2005

Cover photo shows the monument built in Cuba to commemorate the Russians who died when their ship was blown up in 1962 during the Cuban Missiles Crisis © Tim Page/Corbis.
Typeset by Fakenham Photosetting Limited, Fakenham, Norfolk.
Printed in Dubai for Hodder Education, an Hachette UK Company,
338 Euston Road, London, NW1 3BH.